ROBERT S. McNAMARA

OUT OF

Simon and Schuster

New York   London   Toronto   Sydney   Tokyo

THE COLD

New Thinking for
American Foreign and
Defense Policy in the
21st Century

Simon and Schuster
Simon & Schuster Building
Rockefeller Center
1230 Avenue of the Americas
New York, New York 10020

SIMON AND SCHUSTER and colophon are registered
trademarks of Simon & Schuster, Inc.

Designed by Nina D'Amario/Levavi & Levavi
Manufactured in the United States of America

10 9 8 7 6 5 4 3 2 1

Library of Congress Cataloging in Publication data

McNamara, Robert S.
Out of the cold : new thinking for American foreign and defense policy in the 21st century / Robert S. McNamara.
p. cm.
Includes bibliographical references.
1. United States—Foreign relations—Soviet Union.
2. Soviet Union—Foreign relations—United States.   3. Cold
War.   4. United States—Foreign relations—1989–
5. Soviet Union—Foreign relations—1985–   6. United
States—Military policy.   7. Soviet Union—Military policy.   I. Title.
E183.8.S65M38   1989   89–19663
327.73047—dc20   CIP

ISBN 0-671-68983-5

In Memory of Margaret

For forty years she inspired me to pursue the values we shared. It was she who first pointed out to me T. S. Eliot's words from *Four Quartets:*

We shall not cease from exploring
And the end of our exploring
Will be to arrive where we started
And know the place for the first time.

Contents

CONTENTS

CONTENTS

Preface

Since the end of World War II, U.S. foreign and defense policy has focused on containment of what most Westerners saw as a Soviet Union bent on extending its power and ideology over ever larger portions of the globe. Perhaps the threat was never as great as we believed. Certainly we have often overestimated Soviet strengths—political, economic and military—and underestimated our own. In any event, Soviet expansionism has been contained, but the political, economic and social costs to our nation and to the Western world have been enormous, and the risks of military conflict have often been greater than we realized. Must we continue indefinitely on the same path? Are relations among nations fixed in one pattern for all time? Is there now an opportunity to shape a totally different system—

a system of collective security founded on the rule of law—for governing relations among nations during the twenty-first century? I believe there is.

Having been a member of the military forces in the 1940s, an officer of a large industrial enterprise in the 1950s, Secretary of Defense in the 1960s, president of the World Bank in the 1970s, and a participant in innumerable studies of foreign and defense policy in the 1980s, I find that during my entire adult life my perceptions of the world have been dominated by the East–West struggle. It is difficult for me—and I believe for most of us—to conceive of a new pattern of relations among nations. But is it not time, and may we not now have a unique opportunity to do just that?

This slim volume explores that opportunity and outlines the action I believe we should initiate now in order to take advantage of it.

Robert S. McNamara
Washington, D.C.
April 9, 1989

Introduction

The Cold War between East and West—a continuing series of political crises, any one of which had the potential for escalating to military confrontation carrying the risk of destruction of our civilization—has existed for over forty years.

It has led to huge United States expenditures for defense—over two trillion dollars in the eight years 1980–88; it has turned our attention away from urgent domestic problems; it has distorted our relations with other nations; and it has moved us away from our traditional values.

General Secretary Mikhail Gorbachev's public statements have confirmed that the costs to the Soviet Union have been at least as great. On several occasions he has shown a desire to end the conflict. He has stated that war between the superpowers is no longer an acceptable instrument of political change, and he has repeatedly argued that today's problems between East and West must be resolved solely through political means.

Is a world without risk of war between East and West an idle dream, an unrealistic hope? Many—probably most—students of history and geopolitics would claim that it is.

But is such a thought any more inconceivable than Jean Monnet's vision of a United Europe, or Anwar Sadat's initiative to bring peace to Egypt and Israel, or Konrad Adenauer and Charles de Gaulle's determination to ensure peaceful relations between France and Germany after hundreds of years of war, or the dramatic shift in U.S.–Japan relations after World War II, or the termination of the hostile relationship between the United States and China?

Can we visualize a world without the Cold War? What shape would it take? What steps would lead to it? Can we move in that direction without incurring unacceptable risks in the event we fail?

These are questions I will pursue in this essay. In the course of doing so I will examine the origins of the Cold War in the immediate postwar years; trace the evolution of relations between East and West, 1955–85; analyze the impact of the Cold War—its costs—on both of the major adversaries and on the rest of the world; summarize the dramatic shift, in recent years, in the attitudes of the Soviet leaders toward continued conflict with the West, and reflect on the causes and consequences of the change; review the Western response to the Soviet initiatives and propose a far more radical set of moves in both the political and the military spheres; and recognize and discuss potential criticisms of the proposed program.

I will conclude that we do indeed face an opportunity—the greatest in forty years—to bring an end to the Cold War. To fail to grasp it means an indefinite extension of the risk that unintended conflict between East and West will endanger the very survival of our civilization.

I

The Origins of the Cold War:

THE IMMEDIATE POSTWAR YEARS

The answer to the question "Can we end the Cold War?" depends in part on what the Cold War is and how it came about. One's views—certainly my own—of how it evolved have changed over the years. U.S. Soviet scholars are continuing to learn more of why the Soviet leaders acted as they did toward the West and how the behavior of the West influenced those actions. In this chapter, which deals with the beginnings of the Cold War in the immediate postwar years (1945–55), and in the next chapter, which traces the evolution of Soviet foreign policy in the following three decades (1955–85), I shall draw on the writings of those scholars to lay a foundation for considering whether Gorbachev's policies make possible a dramatic shift in East–West relations.

Although even today historians do not agree on the causes, origins and history of the cold War,[1] it is probably safe to say that the character of East–West relations in the immediate postwar period was shaped by (1) the long and tense negotiations, at the end of World War II, over the division of Europe and the composition and character of the regimes that would govern postwar European states; (2) the West's interpretation of the Soviet Marxist-Leninist ideology; and (3) a continuing series of contentious issues, inside and outside of Europe, which contributed to the spiral of mutual suspicion and hostility.

Spheres of Influence: The Basis for the Division of Europe

An examination of the origins of the Cold War—the Soviet and American national-security calculations that gave rise to it and the misperceptions that fueled it— must begin with Soviet–American diplomacy during the final years of World War II. Beginning with the Teheran Conference of the Big Three—Winston Churchill, Franklin Roosevelt and Joseph Stalin—in November 1943, the Allies sought to shape the postwar order. Among the most troublesome issues even in 1943 were those that dealt with the future political makeup of the soon-to-be-liberated European states. Little progress was made at Teheran on such political issues, as the Allies' paramount concern was still the military defeat of Nazi Germany. A year later, however, political concerns had come to the fore. British Prime Minister

Winston Churchill traveled to Moscow in October 1944 to lay out the initial outlines of the political order in postwar Europe.

At one of their Moscow meetings, Churchill handed Stalin an offer of "spheres of influence" in Europe.[2] On that famous slip of paper, Churchill suggested that Western and Soviet influence in Romania would be divided 90–10 in favor of the Soviets; in Greece, 90–10 in favor of the West; in Bulgaria, 75–25 in favor of the USSR; and in Yugoslavia, 50–50. It was, of course, unclear to both Churchill and Stalin what these figures actually meant. How, for example, could influence in Romania be divided 90–10 in favor of Moscow? Moreover, the case of Poland, the one that was to cause the most trouble among the Allies, was not even mentioned. In any event, Stalin signaled his agreement with the concept and with the figures by placing a small blue check mark on the sheet of paper.

While this spheres-of-influence approach may have seemed an obvious one for two leaders of nations with long histories of empire, it was explicitly denounced by virtually all American policymakers. The American view of the postwar world foresaw the internationalization of security, and its guarantee by international organizations. Spheres of influence were abhorrent to the American ethic of the day. Writing of the American view of spheres of influence, A. W. DePorte noted:

> No one at the decision-making level saw the merit, as Churchill did, of striking the best deal possible with the Russians as the preface to establishing the postwar

order. Certainly no one thought of an understanding on spheres of influence as a prerequisite for doing so. On the contrary, such an approach was seen as the most basic challenge to the American vision of the postwar period.[3]

Roosevelt never fully surrendered to the spheres-of-influence approach; until the end of his life, he was a staunch supporter of the idea that international organizations would keep the peace and maintain order in the postwar world. But by the end of the war, the determining factor in the development of European polities appeared to be simply the location of the occupation armies. Those states liberated and occupied by the Western Allies went on to develop strong and secure democracies, and, with very few exceptions, those countries occupied at the end of the war by the Soviet Army eventually established Communist rule. In the words of DePorte, "It has turned out to be self-evident that nothing is as effective in orienting a country as an occupying army."[4]

At the time, it was feared the Soviets would move to go beyond the line of occupation. Dire predictions of the Soviet Army marching to the English Channel were common in the immediate postwar period, at least in the United States. In reality, however, the Soviets were even less interested in war, and less capable of fighting one, than the Western countries. After four years of an enormously destructive war in which over twenty million citizens lost their lives, almost two-thirds of Soviet industrial capacity was destroyed, and over half of the productive agricultural land was overrun, Stalin, it is now clear, had no intention of launching a war against the West. Highest on his list of postwar priorities was ensuring Soviet security and—if possible—increasing Soviet power, prestige, and influence without war.

Soviet Ideology and the Cold War

It is perhaps on this issue that the greatest misperceptions of Soviet intentions arose among Western policymakers. Much of this confusion was the result of a poor understanding of the content and significance of Soviet "ideology." While it is true that Marxist-Leninist thinking puts great emphasis on the notions of "class struggle" and even on the importance of conflict and violence, by the late 1920s Marxists did not believe that the export of violence was necessary for the spreading of socialism—certainly they do not believe so today. On the contrary, because Marxists had confidence in the eventual triumph of socialism, their ideology counseled patience in the face of opposition.

In order for the Soviet state to survive the period before the world revolution, Lenin established the concept of "peaceful coexistence." Although he considered peaceful coexistence to be a temporary tactic, designed to provide Soviet Russia the time to strengthen itself, Lenin clearly allowed for the possibility of socialists and capitalists existing side by side. He never believed that the Soviets were compelled to make war on the capitalists.

Only a few years after Lenin's death in 1924, Stalin established a new orthodoxy in the Soviet Union, building on the concept of "peaceful coexistence." Stalin's doctrine of "socialism in one country" held that the Soviet Union, even if it was the only socialist state on the globe, could survive for as long as necessary as it awaited the "inevitable" world revolution. In Stalin's time the date of the world revolution was pushed decades into the future.

By the late 1950s, and continuing through the Brezhnev period, peaceful coexistence was considered a broad, long-term strategy that allowed the Soviet Union to continue the "class struggle" with the West under conditions in which nuclear weapons threatened the very existence of the Soviet state. The future world revolution was discussed as taking place in another "historical epoch." Now, under Gorbachev, peaceful coexistence is not regarded as a transient stage of Soviet development, but as a long-term condition of East–West relations. It is this current Soviet view of the concept that allows for the possibility of the genuine stabilization of East–West political relations that I will discuss in Chapter V.[5]

While Soviet ideology, therefore, did not compel Soviet leaders to undertake violence against the West, it did counsel them to take advantage of opportunities to spread socialism around the world. And there is no doubt that during the immediate aftermath of World

War II Stalin ceaselessly pursued every opportunity presented to him. The traditional interpretaton of the Cold War holds that "Russia's striving for power and influence far in excess of its reasonable security requirements was the primary source of the conflict," and at the same time that the Western—and particularly American—failure to respond quickly to Stalin's moves was "an important secondary" cause.[6]

This assessment is probably accurate as far as it goes (though it leaves out the important factor of interacting misperceptions), and it does not rely on an ideological explanation. If anything, Soviet ideology at the end of World War II counseled patience and caution; any reasonable assessment of Soviet power at the time would indicate that violently exporting revolution would be doomed to failure and could even result in the destruction of the Soviet state. Students of the Cold War agree that the first Soviet priority was to establish secure frontiers in Eastern Europe; they also tend to agree that any Russian government, tsarist or socialist, regardless of ideology, would have sought security in much the same way that Stalin did:

Any Russian government, after such a war and the defeat of Germany, would have annexed border territory which it had lost only twenty years before, just as it would have restored the pre-1905 status quo in the Far East once the defeat of Japan made possible the recovery of its colonial position in Manchuria and northern Korea.[7]

It seems likely, then, that Stalin was driven to guarantee the subservience of East European regimes, not because of the demands of a prescriptive ideology, but because his view of security demanded it and the opportunities were present.

The United States vigorously denounced such moves, but found itself powerless to prevent them. The fear was growing in Washington that Moscow was building toward a clash with Western Europe and with the United States itself. For its part, Moscow interpreted the U.S. opposition to its activities in Eastern Europe as a direct threat to the security of the Soviet state. The London Conference of Foreign Ministers which took place from September 11 to October 2, 1945, reflected the misunderstandings and ended in acrimony, without even issuing a communiqué. U.S. Secretary of State James F. Byrnes pressed Soviet Foreign Minister Molotov on demands that the Soviets reorganize the Bulgarian and Romanian governments. According to Barton J. Bernstein,

He [Byrnes] would not acknowledge and perhaps could not understand the dilemma of his policy: that he was supporting free elections in areas (particularly in Rumania) where the resulting governments would probably be hostile to the Soviet Union, and yet he was arguing that democracy in Eastern Europe was compatible with Soviet demands for security. Unable to accept that Byrnes might be naive, Molotov questioned the secretary's sincerity and charged that he wanted governments unfriendly to the Soviet Union. From this,

Byrnes could only conclude later, "It seemed that the Soviet Union was determined to dominate Europe."[8]

Each side, therefore, poorly understood the motivations of the other. The difficulty was that Soviet moves that Moscow saw as defensive were regarded as extremely aggressive by the United States, and vice versa. Moreover, the United States refused to see parallels between Moscow's support of socialism in Eastern Europe and the West's armed defense of democracy in Western Europe:

> Byrnes would not admit the similarity between Russian behavior in Rumania and British action in Greece. As part of the terms of his agreement with Churchill, Stalin had allowed the British to suppress a revolutionary force in Greece, and as a result the Greek government could not be accurately interpreted as broadly representative nor as a product of democratic procedures.[9]

While one can argue the relative merits of the armed imposition of democracy as opposed to the violent establishment of socialism, the Soviets were correct in drawing the parallel, especially in view of Churchill and Roosevelt's agreement for 90–10 divisions of influence in Romania and Greece.

Germany

At the heart of the discussions of the Big Three on the structure of postwar Europe was the question of

29

the future of Germany. In early 1943, the U.S. State Department opposed the partition of Germany. Officials believed that dismemberment would increase German antipathy to any peace arrangement and would not strengthen European peace and security. The State Department argued that a disarmed Germany would guarantee peace better than a partitioned one. When the Big Three met at Teheran in November of 1943, however, Roosevelt proposed the dismemberment of Germany. In part, this was an effort to strengthen U.S. relations with Stalin, who was known to favor harsh punishment for Germany. As Roosevelt foresaw, Stalin reacted extremely enthusiastically to the proposal of a divided Germany.[10]

During the decade after 1943, however, the British, the French and the Americans found very few areas of agreement with their Soviet counterparts on issues relating to postwar Germany. Contention over such problems as future German borders, reparations to be exacted from the four occupation zones, interaction among the zones, and a 1944 U.S. plan to "pastoralize" Germany and convert it to a wholly agrarian economy all contributed to the increasingly bitter and rancorous discussions.[11]

The negotiations on the structure of possible German governments were enormously prolonged and complicated, and very little was resolved by the four powers acting in concert. In June of 1947, the Soviets unilaterally established the economic administration of their zone and drastically curtailed contact with the other zones of occupation. In February 1948 (the same month as the Communist coup in Czechoslovakia), France, Britain and the United States opened negotiations in London on the formation of a West German state. The following month, in response, the Soviets walked out of the four-power Control Council, and in June the decision to establish the West German state was announced.

A week later, on June 18, the three Western powers announced the imminent introduction of a currency reform in their zones. The Soviets followed with a currency reform in their zone and in all of Berlin. The Western powers brought the new West German currency into West Berlin on June 23, and the Soviets responded the following day by blockading the western zones of the city. They closed the overland routes into the city and cut off its electrical supply.

The Berlin blockade of 1948–49 was clearly an attempt to force the West out of Berlin and pressure the West into negotiations on larger German issues. Above all, Stalin hoped to prevent the establishment of a unified, armed West German state firmly allied to the United States and Western Europe. In August of 1948, he met with Western envoys and demanded negotiations on reparations, the demilitarization of Germany, the formation of a German state, and a peace treaty with Germany. By this time, the West was both more confident of its own position and more suspicious of Soviet motives. No concessions were offered. The United States airlifted supplies into West Berlin for almost a full year, and the blockade was lifted in May 1949. The Federal Republic of Germany (West Germany) was established as an independent state in September 1949.

Contentious Issues Outside Europe

Territorial issues and the nature of East and West European governments were the primary issues in the immediate postwar period. Directly related to these, however, was the process undertaken by each superpower to expand and consolidate its bloc outside the central arena of Europe. Most important, the Soviets were pressuring the governments of Turkey and Greece immediately after the war. Ultimately these conflicts were resolved in the West's favor, but only after the United States had replaced Britain as the protector of those nations.

The British informed the United States in February 1947 that they could no longer support the defense of Greece and Turkey. The British Treasury, depleted by the war, was in no shape to offer security guarantees to distant states. As a result, on March 12, 1947, the Truman Doctrine was proclaimed, promising U.S. support to "free peoples who are resisting attempted subjugation by armed minorities or by outside pressures." The Soviets interpreted the Truman Doctrine as an effort by the United States to involve itself in an area of the world far beyond its traditional sphere. Since the United States could have no defensive reason for involvement in Greece and Turkey, in the Soviet view American motives must have been offensive.

One small event on the periphery of Europe took place in early 1946. In a speech in February of that year, Soviet Foreign Minister Vyacheslav Molotov demanded that the Soviet Union be allowed to take control of the trusteeship over the former Italian colony of Tripolitania in Africa; the other victorious powers were dividing up the trusteeships of the Axis states, and the Soviet Union felt entitled to its share of the spoils. Not surprisingly, the Western powers vehemently opposed the Soviet initiative, and the issue was quietly dropped. DePorte contends that this exchange revealed a major difference in the perceptions of the states involved: the Soviets saw themselves as a world power, entitled to everything that that distinction implies, while the Western powers were completely unwilling to bestow this status on the USSR. "This small episode—the Soviet demand and the Western reponse to it—highlights the deeper and long-lasting problem of Soviet claims to, and Western reluctance to accept, the full implications in status terms of the USSR's position as a *world* power."[12]

China. Perhaps the most important event outside Europe was the Communist victory in the Chinese Civil War in October 1949. Most analysts agree that Stalin probably encouraged the Chinese Communists to move slowly in the period 1946–49, but Mao was not willing to listen to counsels of restraint. His victory in 1949 surprised not only the West but almost certainly Stalin as well. As a result of the Communist takeover of China, however, the Western perception of the "Communist threat" was drastically increased. The specter of monolithic world Communism was perceived as more aggressive, and more successful, than ever. But this perception of world Communism as completely monolithic was—as we know now with hindsight—inaccurate. Although the Sino–Soviet break was not brought into the open until 1960, strains in the relationship between Stalin and Mao began even before the Communist Chinese took power in 1949. Moreover, Josip Broz Tito of Yugoslavia had broken with Stalin in 1948, demonstrating that there were indeed deep cracks in the Communist monolith.

U.S. Economic Policy, the Cold War and Containment

By 1947, Communists were in complete control in Poland, Bulgaria, Romania and Yugoslavia, and would soon take unopposed control in Czechoslovakia and Hungary. Germany was inexorably dividing itself along East–West lines, and, as I have noted, in March of 1947 the United States promulgated the Truman Doctrine. In addition to these political divisions, in the postwar period the United States initiated economic policies that appeared to the Soviets to be designed to isolate and threaten the Communist states of Europe.

Most important among these was the Marshall Plan for the reconstruction and development of Europe. The plan was introduced by Secretary of State George C.

Marshall at a speech at Harvard University in June 1947 in which he declared that U.S. policy was "directed not against any country or doctrine but against hunger, poverty, desperation and chaos." Indeed, all the countries of Europe, including the Soviet Union and its allies, were invited to participate. This invitation may have been disingenuous, however, as the U.S. Congress made clear that much of the support for the plan came from those who viewed it as a means to respond to the perceived Soviet threat to Europe.

Moscow's response to the Marshall Plan was to create in September the Communist Information Bureau, or Cominform, an organization through which Stalin imposed his will on East European states and West European Communist parties. Both American and Soviet analysts point to the creation of the Marshall Plan and the Cominform as the events that solidified the division of Europe into two hostile camps. Adam Ulam notes, "With the Marshall Plan the cold war assumes the character of position warfare. Both sides become frozen in mutual unfriendliness."[13] And according to DePorte:

There could have been no clearer declaration of ideological war between the two halves of Europe and their superpower leaders. The line of division expressed in Europe between those countries which took part in the Marshall Plan and those which joined the Cominform struck contemporaries as signifying a basic division and alignment going far beyond the actual programs of either.[14]

From this division of Europe naturally flowed the idea of confining Soviet influence within the sphere that the USSR had already carved out for itself. In July 1947, after the declaration of the Truman Doctrine and the launching of the Marshall Plan, George F. Kennan published a famous article in the journal *Foreign Affairs* under the pseudonym "X." It was an elegant analysis of the "Sources of Soviet Conduct," and it made famous the term that was to characterize U.S. policy toward the Soviet Union for the next four decades—"containment."

Kennan asserted that three fundamental elements of Stalinist thinking were instrumental in shaping Soviet domestic politics and Soviet foreign policy:

First, Stalin could brook no opposition at home or within the East European satellite countries: "Now it lies in the nature of the mental world of the Soviet leaders, as well as in the character of their ideology, that no opposition to them can be officially recognized as having any merit or justification whatsoever."[15]

Second, the Soviets require the image of a hostile enemy to justify foreign and domestic repression; Kennan referred to the Soviets' "cultivation of the semi-myth of implacable foreign hostility."[16]

Third, although Stalin could not be optimistic about the results of a potential U.S.-Soviet war, during the early days of the Cold War, his world view was founded on the certainty of conflicts of interests between socialism and capitalism. Regarding the Soviet vision of "innate antagonism between capitalism and socialism," Kennan wrote:

We have seen how deeply that concept has become imbedded in foundations of Soviet power. It has profound implications for Russia's conduct as a member of international society. It means that there can never be on Moscow's side any sincere assumption of a community of aims between the Soviet Union and powers which are regarded as capitalist.[17]

Kennan argued that the Soviet Union was far weaker than the United States and that "Soviet society may well contain deficiencies which will eventually weaken its own total potential." He correctly predicted that the ultimate failure of the Soviet economy, in contrast to the health and vitality of capitalist states, would drive the Soviet Union toward reform. The Soviets, he argued, would have to improve their economy, if only to present a better image to the developing world:

> It is difficult to see how these deficiencies can be corrected at an early date by a tired and dispirited population working largely under the shadow of fear and compulsion. And as long as they are not overcome, Russia will remain economically a vulnerable, and in a certain sense an impotent nation, capable of exporting its enthusiasm and of radiating the strange charm of its primitive political vitality but unable to back up those articles of export by the real evidences of material power and prosperity.[18]

Pointing to economic deficiencies, Kennan argued that "Soviet power . . . bears within it the seeds of its own decay, and . . . the sprouting of these seeds is well advanced."[19] He also argued that the relative economic strength of the capitalist countries would provide an example to the world and might cause a waning of the influence of Communism. "Even the failure of the United States to experience the early economic depression which the ravens of the Red Square have been predicting with such complacent confidence . . . would have deep and important repercussions throughout the Communist world."[20]

Kennan did not perceive a military threat from the Soviet Union in 1947. He was well aware that the USSR was prostrate after World War II and had no plans for an attack on Western Europe. The threat that Kennan did percieve, and the Soviet actions that he sought to "contain," were ideological-political in nature. Pro-Communist parties were active in France and Italy after the war, securing a number of cabinet positions for their leaders. In addition, the Soviet Union called for major strikes and uprisings by Communists in an effort to undermine French and Italian support for the Marshall Plan.

In a 1987 discussion of "containment," Kennan explained that "there seemed to be a danger that communist parties subservient to Moscow might seize power in some of the major Western European countries, notably Italy and France, and possibly in Japan." "I felt," he argued, "that if Moscow should be successful in taking over any of those major Western countries, or Japan, by ideological-political intrigue and penetration, this would be a defeat for us, and a blow to our national security, fully as serious as would have been a German victory in the war that had just ended."[21]

Kennan's view of containment did not argue that the Soviet Union required expansion to survive. He did not believe that containment itself would directly lead to a Soviet collapse. Rather, he believed that if Soviet ideological-political expansion could be checked, the Soviets would be forced to confront their own internal deficiencies. And, as a result of examining those deficiencies, Soviet legitimacy would decline until Moscow could improve its own domestic situation. The recent statements and policies of the Soviet leadership clearly indicate that Kennan's reasoning was accurate.

Kennan himself believes that his article was misinterpreted at the time of its publication; American policymakers exaggerated the military threat emanating from the Soviet Union and overemphasized "military containment." In a series of misperceptions which is now a familiar theme of this narrative, each side saw the other's action as hostile and aggressive. An official Soviet interpretation of the postwar international scene describes the Marshall Plan as part of a U.S. policy of "world domination": "The new course of American foreign policy meant a return to the old anti-Soviet course, designed to unloose war and forcibly to institute world domination by Britain and the United States."[22]

The Cominform's founding declaration claimed that "imperialism" was on the offensive according to a "general plan" for "global expansion,"[23] while the United States Embassy in Moscow called the Cominform declaration "a declaration of political and economic war against [the] US and everything [the] US stands for in world affairs."[24] In fact it was not a declaration of war; the Soviets saw themselves on the defensive and the West as on the offensive. The text of the declaration states that the task of Communists is to "close ranks . . . to frustrate the plan of imperialist aggression." Communist parties must not "let themselves be intimidated and blackmailed."[25]

These misperceptions were based largely on misunderstandings of the "ideology" of the other side. Policymakers in the United States believed that Soviet ideology required aggressive Soviet expansion. As discussed above, Soviet ideology surely expected a worldwide expansion of socialism, but it did not prescribe aggressive Soviet moves to make that expansion come about. U.S. officials, however, believing that the Soviets were compelled to expand by some all-powerful belief system, tended to see such expansion where it was not necessarily present.

On the other hand, the Soviets were equally suspicious of the perceived U.S. plans for "world domination." There was no explanation in Soviet thinking for a capitalist power that would spend billions of dollars merely to save the economies of other capitalist countries. Since these countries would sooner or later become competitors with the United States, the United States could not possibly be seeking to build them up with no strings attached. U.S. aims, in the Soviet view, must have been military, and must have been intended to prevent further Soviet gains and take away those already achieved by Moscow.

Moscow perceived three additional U.S. initiatives to be intended as economic pressure on the Soviet Union. First was Truman's decision, immediately after V-E Day, to cut off Lend-Lease aid to the USSR. Second was the apparent U.S. reneging on agreements on reparations from Germany. Roosevelt had agreed at Yalta that the amount of $20 billion should be the "basis of negotiation" and that approximately half of that sum would go to Moscow. But at the meeting of the reparations committee in June 1945, the United States retreated from this position. The compromise arrived at in Potsdam fell far short of Soviet expectations.

The third instance of perceived economic pressure was the unusual treatment given to a Soviet postwar loan application. The Soviets had applied for a $6 billion loan from the United States at the beginning of 1945. In Washington in May, Molotov asked about the status of the application. The answer did not come until August, when the Soviets were advised that their application had been improperly submitted and that they should reapply to the U.S. Export-Import Bank. The Soviets then applied for a loan of $1 billion. They raised the issue again at the December foreign ministers' conference and received no satisfactory reply. On March 1, 1946, the State Department reported that the August application had been misplaced, but that negotiations could now open.[26] The matter was eventually dropped, and the Soviets never received the loan.

The Evolution of Western Security Arrangements

Although Moscow felt that the United States was seeking to impose economic pressure on the USSR, the Soviets were even more concerned about developments in Western security policy. The first step toward integration of West European and U.S. defense efforts was taken in the March 1947 Anglo–French Treaty of Dunkirk, which established a mutual-defense arrangement between the two countries. The arrangement was directed mostly at what the parties perceived as a possible future threat from Germany rather than from the USSR. As discussed above, however, events in 1947 went a long way toward solidifying the divisions between East and West. The likelihood of a permanently divided Europe was growing, and with it grew the importance of West European economic recovery. In the view of virtually all West Europeans, Germany was going to have to play a part in that recovery, as well as in guaranteeing the security of Western Europe.

The Treaty of Dunkirk was therefore expanded into the Treaty of Brussels of March 17, 1948, a month after the Czechoslovak coup. The Brussels Treaty added the Benelux countries to Britain and France, and was clearly directed at the USSR. Even at the time of its signing, the treaty was viewed as paving the way for an American guarantee of West European security. In July 1948, a month after the imposition of the Berlin blockade, negotiations began on establishing a formal alliance with the United States. Nine months later, on April 4, 1949, the North Atlantic Treaty was signed by the original five signatories of the Brussels Treaty plus Canada, Denmark, Iceland, Italy, Norway, Portugal and the United States.

The following year, in April 1950, the U.S. National Security Council approved a document that interpreted Soviet behavior in the darkest possible light and advised an enormous buildup of U.S. armed forces before the Soviets could undertake a preemptive attack on the United States. The document, known as NSC-68, claimed that Moscow sought "to impose its absolute authority over the rest of the world," a goal which required "the ultimate elimination of any effective opposition to [Moscow's] authority." To achieve their aims, according to NSC-68, the Soviets would have to effect "the complete subversion or forcible destruction of the machinery of government and structure of society in the countries of the non-Soviet world and their replacement by an apparatus and structure subservient to and controlled from the Kremlin."[27]

As if to confirm the analysis in NSC-68, the Soviet-backed regime in North Korea attacked the pro-American regime in the South in June, only two months after the dissemination of NSC-68. The sudden nature of the attack caught Americans by surprise. It appeared to be the quintessential act of Communist aggression to date. And indeed there is no question that the Korean War certainly was an example of naked aggression on the part of the North Koreans, with at least the tacit consent of Joseph Stalin. But the attack on South Korea proved to be neither the prelude to World War III—as many Americans believed at the time—nor a Soviet feint in Asia designed to draw down the number of U.S. troops in Europe. In a number of ways, the Korean War, like other episodes in the Cold War, was the result of genuine conflicts of geopolitical interests that were fueled and exacerbated by poor judgments of the other side's intentions.

For example, in a now famous speech before the National Press Club in Washington, Secretary of State Dean Acheson in January 1950 gave the impression that the United States would not defend South Korea if the latter state were attacked. In reality, however, Acheson was discussing the U.S. defense perimeter in the event of a *world* war; by no means did he state or imply that the defense of South Korea, per se, was unimportant to the United States. Evidently North Korean and Soviet leaders made fundamental errors in their interpretations of Acheson's speech.

The evidence suggests that the Soviets themselves may have been surprised by the North Korean attack— at least by its timing—and by the U.S. response. When the United Nations Security Council met on the very day of the North Korean attack to consider a response, the Soviet delegate was not present. On orders from the Soviet government, he had been boycotting the Security Council since January of 1950 because of the U.S. and other states' opposition to replacing the Council's Nationalist Chinese representative with a delegate from the People's Republic of China. As a result of the Soviet delegate's absence, the U.S. resolution declaring the North Korean attack a "breach of the peace," which cleared the way for the deployment of UN forces in Korea, passed unanimously.[28]

According to Kennan, once again the United States and the Soviet Union saw each other as motivated primarily by aggressive, offensive designs. The Korean War was read in Washington as "the beginning of the final Soviet push for world conquest; whereas the active American military response, provoked by this Soviet move, appeared in Moscow as a threat to the Soviet position both in Manchuria and in eastern Sibera."[29]

By the end of 1952, with the Korean War having settled into a stalemate, the integration of the Western security system was continuing. Under the provisions of the European Defense Community (EDC), West Germany was to be allowed to remilitarize, and its forces were to be integrated into an all-EDC force. As envisioned by the planners of the EDC, independent national armed forces would not exist in Europe; all troops would be integrated under the EDC structure. Although the French were among the strongest supporters of the EDC in its earliest stages, the French National Assembly on August 30, 1954, refused to ratify its creation. Two months later, however, under the terms of the Paris Agreement of October 1954, the Federal Republic of Germany was granted membership in the North Atlantic Treaty Organization. Only then did the Soviets see the need to create the Warsaw Treaty Organization

(WTO, or Warsaw Pact), which was established in May of 1955.

In addition to the defense arrangements with Western Europe, Moscow was troubled by two related developments in American security policy during the Cold War. The first was what Soviets called U.S. "pactomania" and "capitalist encirclement"; the second was the apparent U.S. willingness to develop the weapons and strategies required to launch a "nuclear first strike" on the Soviet Union.

The signing of the North Atlantic Treaty was followed by a long series of bilateral and multilateral security agreements by the Truman and Eisenhower Administrations:

> Mutual defense treaties with Japan (1950), the Philippines (1951), Korea (1953), Nationalist China (1954); security treaties with Australia and New Zealand (ANZUS) (1951), and with nations interested in Southeast Asia (SEATO) (1954); bilateral agreements to resist aggression with Iran, Turkey, and Pakistan (1959) . . . . When President Nixon took office in 1969, the United States was party to mutual defense agreements with some forty-three countries.[30]

Since, in the Soviet view, such a widespread network of agreements could not have a purely defensive *raison d'être*, American motives toward the Soviet Union must have been offensive and aggressive.

Confirming and exacerbating this Soviet perception were ambiguous hints from Washington—interpreted in the worst possible light by the Soviets—that the United States was considering a nuclear first strike on the Soviet Union:

In a January 1946 memorandum, General Leslie R. Groves, the director of the Manhattan Project, urged that the United States initiate a nuclear attack against any "aggressor nation" about to acquire the bomb.[31]

Fleetwood, the U.S. war plan readied by the fall of 1948, "proposed that virtually the entire US arsenal of atomic bombs be dropped on Russian cities in the first month of the war. Another option in the plan was an 'atomic blitz,' utilizing every American atomic bomb and bomber in a single cataclysmic attack."[32]

NSC-68, the document approved by the National Security Council in 1950, declared that "the military advantages of landing the first blow . . . require us to be on the alert in order to strike with our full weight as soon as we are attacked, and, if possible, before the Soviet blow is actually delivered. . . . In the initial phases of an atomic war, the advantages of initiative and surprise would be very great."[33]

In the fall of 1950, Navy Secretary Francis Matthews suggested that Americans become the first "aggressors for peace."[34]

The End of the Stalin Era

The Soviets had clearly made great advances in the period between the end of World War II and the death of Joseph Stalin in March of 1953. East Europe and China had been Communized, and few doubted that the USSR had achieved the status of a true world power. Nonetheless, many of Stalin's attempts at strengthening Soviet security were unquestionably counterproductive. The Berlin blockade of 1948–49, for example, surely strengthened Western support for the creation of West Germany, the establishment of an anti-Soviet Western alliance and the inclusion of a rearmed Germany in that alliance. Similarly, the Korean War justified and accelerated rearmament of Germany and contributed to the enormous increase in U.S. defense spending after the approval of NSC-68. If Stalin sought to postpone or prevent the rearming of Germany and its integration into a Western security system—and there is abundant evidence that he hoped to do exactly that—his own policies undermined his goals.

In addition, the very manner of Soviet policy behavior under Stalinism increased Western suspicion. According to George Kennan,

That behavior remained marked at all times, in one degree or another, by features—disrespect for the truth; claims to infallibility; excessive secrecy; excessive armaments; ruthless domination of satellite peoples; and

repressive policies at home—that were bound to arouse
distaste and resentment in American opinion, and thus
to feed and sustain the distorted image of Soviet Russia . . .[35]

After Stalin's death, the new Soviet leadership moved
quickly to improve its image and its relations with the
West. "At present," First Secretary Georgi Malenkov
declared on March 15, 1953, "there is no litigious or
unsolved question which could not be settled by peaceful means on the basis of mutual agreement with the
countries concerned. This concerns our relations with
all states, including the United States of America." Andrey Gromyko echoed this theme at the United Nations
on March 26, and Moscow called for faster programs
in the negotiations on a Korean armistice, which was
eventually signed in August.[36]

In a speech that August, Malenkov listed the recent
steps undertaken by the Soviet government to reduce
international tensions. As described by Ulam, Malenkov
could offer impressive evidence of a new Soviet attitude
toward international relations:

> The Soviet government had relinquished its territorial
> claims in Turkey. It extended a hand of friendship to
> Turkey and Iran. It re-established diplomatic relations
> with Israel. Ambassadors had been exchanged with Yu-
> goslavia and Greece. Malenkov spoke flatteringly of
> India [and] held out a prospect of friendship to Japan
> once she freed herself from American tutelage. British
> public opinion was praised.[37]

As further evidence of the new Soviet attitude toward foreign policy, the Soviet leadership in May 1955 did what few observers considered possible. Moscow signed the Austrian peace treaty, which provided for the complete withdrawal of all foreign troops and absolute neutrality for Austria. Many analysts agree that the Soviets accepted the withdrawal of their troops as a means to persuade East and West Germans that unification and neutralization were still possible in their country. But if that was the Soviet goal, the process of arming West Germany and integrating it into the Western defense structure had gone much too far for it to be a realistic possibility.[38]

Nonetheless, the Soviets had gone a long way toward rejecting the Stalinist foundations of Soviet foreign policy. They seemed to believe that cooperative solutions to problems were possible and appeared to recognize that unilateral undertakings can sometimes result in greater costs than benefits. In any event, because of the relative calm on the international scene, and the new Soviet attitude toward international relations, many observers believed that 1955 would mark the dawn of a new era in U.S.–Soviet relations. The "good feeling" that resulted from the four-power summit in July 1955—the so-called "spirit of Geneva"—seemed to offer optimism for the years to come.

II

The Evolution of East–West Relations, 1955–85

The Soviet withdrawal from Austria finally established the outlines of postwar Europe, and, as I have said, it appeared to be ushering in a period of calm in international politics. However, this chapter will show that in the three decades following 1955 the Soviet Union moved aggressively either when it perceived threats to its security or when opportunities for low-cost expansion presented themselves. When threats and opportunities were absent, the Soviet Union tended to behave rather passively on the international scene.

Khrushchev, Eastern Europe and Suez

Although the U.S.–Soviet relationship was still unquestionably dominated by Cold War thinking in 1955, tension appeared to be relaxing after the death of Stalin in 1953, and relations were improving after the four-power summit in Geneva in July of 1955. The first major postsummit event to send tremors through U.S.–Soviet relations took place in February 1956, when Nikita Khrushchev made two famous speeches to the Twentieth Congress of the Communist Party of the Soviet Union. Khrushchev's speeches contained three groundbreaking innovations. First, of course, were his shattering denunciations of the brutality and criminality of Joseph Stalin. Second, Khrushchev put forth the new ideological proposition that war between the capitalists and the socialists was no longer "fatalistically inevitable." He argued that "peaceful coexistence," Lenin's temporary survival tactic, could become a permanent feature of Soviet foreign policy. Third, Khrushchev advocated "separate national roads to socialism," rejecting the earlier Stalinist requirement of blind obedience in Eastern Europe.

Each of these innovations had a powereful impact on Communist parties around the world. In other Communist nations, according to Adam Ulam, the speech's "effect was shattering. Their leaders were virtually cast adrift."[1] Every leader of every socialist country had been trained under Stalin's all-powerful mythology. In one blow, not only was Khrushchev stripping Stalin of his mantle of infallibility, but he made Stalin look like a cowardly, murderous lunatic. As a result, the legitimacy of the East European states and their leaders, imposed by Stalin himself, was seriously threatened; riots and unrest broke out in Eastern Europe almost immediately.

The two most troubling countries, from the point of view of the Soviets, were Poland and Hungary. To calm the unrest in Poland, Khrushchev removed from prison and installed in the top party position a former Polish leader, Wladyslaw Gomulka, who was able to manage the turmoil successfully. Gomulka in the summer and fall of 1956 was able to achieve three goals, each of which was necessary to prevent a Soviet invasion: he kept power over events in the hands of the Communist Party; he maintained Poland's alliance with the USSR; and he retained the loyalty of the Polish people to its leadership.

The difficulty of Gomulka's achievement is illustrated by the fact that the Hungarian leadership was completely unable to perform any of the three vital tasks. On October 30 and 31, 1956, in response to enormous popular pressure, Hungarian Prime Minister Imre Nagy declared that Hungary would no longer be a one-party state, would declare its neutrality and would leave the Warsaw Pact. By November 4, Moscow launched a massive attack on Budapest and other Hungarian cities. The rebellion was crushed by Soviet tanks, and Moscow installed its puppet, Janos Kadar, in the leadership of the Hungarian party.

For many years previous to 1956, the United States had made it clear that it would seek to take advantage of opportunities to aid those Communist states that sought to distance themselves from Moscow or even reject their Communist regimes. At least in its early formulations, for example, the declared U.S. goal of the "rollback" of Communism was taken very seriously by the Soviet Union. A 1949 NSC document declared that the United States should seek to place "greater emphasis on the offensive to consider whether we cannot do more to cause the elimination or at least a reduction of predominant Soviet influence in the satellite states of Eastern Europe."[2] The threat was exposed as hollow, however, when the West failed to respond to major uprisings in 1953 in East Germany and to the events in Poland and Hungary in 1956. It is difficult to conceive of a proportionate and prudent U.S. military response to the events of 1953 and 1956. Indeed, implementing the doctrine of "rollback" was probably never possible. But it is also probably true that the lack of U.S. response in 1953 led Soviet leaders to be somewhat bolder in their treatment of Hungarians in 1956. Similarly, the inability of Western forces to contain, much less roll back, Soviet tanks in 1956 must have influenced Soviet thinking during the invasion of Czechoslovakia in 1968.

Although the West condemned the Soviet Union for its invasion of Hungary, at the very same time Britain and France were cooperating with Israel in an invasion of Egypt. On October 29, 1956, Israel attacked Egypt. The British and the French, as had been planned in advance, joined the fighting in an effort to regain control over the Suez Canal, which Gamal Abdel Nasser had nationalized in July of 1956. British and French landings in Egypt began on November 5, but by the following day strong pressure from President Eisenhower forced the two powers to curtail their operations. In the end, the operation was an enormous failure, resulting in the closing of the canal, the destruction of oil installations owned by Western states, and a precipitous drop in British and French prestige and power in the region. Moreover, it served as effective, if unintentional, cover for the Soviet operation in Hungary.

Arab nationalism was fueled by the Suez crisis, and many Arab states tended to attribute the failure of the British and French operation not to American pressure, but to the Soviet nuclear threats that were put forth as the operation was winding down. This combination of Arab nationalism and increasing Soviet prestige in the region led to the promulgation of the Eisenhower Doctrine in January 1957. The Doctrine took the form of a congressional resolution promising American military and economic assistance to any country that requested it in order "to secure and protect the territorial integrity and political independence of such nations, requesting such aid, against overt armed aggression from any nation controlled by International Communism."[3] Perceived threats of such aggression led to increased American arms shipments to Jordan and Syria throughout 1957 and 1958 and to the landing of U.S. Marines in Lebanon in 1958.

The Tension of 1958–60

U.S.–Soviet tension continued to rise in October 1957, when the Soviet Union became the first nation to launch an artificial earth satellite. Americans had long regarded the Soviet Union as technologically backward and incapable of any important feats of science or engineering. The launching of Sputnik changed those prejudices overnight, however, and they were replaced by increased fear of Soviet intentions and capabilities. The Soviets had detonated their first atomic bomb in 1949 and exploded a hydrogen device four years later. If the Soviets could now launch an earth satellite, it was reasoned in Washington, they could just as easily launch an intercontinental ballistic missile (ICBM) directed at the United States.

In 1958, tension and conflict continued. In August, the Communist Chinese began heavy shelling of two islands in the Taiwan Strait, Quemoy and Matsu. The shelling, designed perhaps to reduce the American commitment to the defense of Taiwan and extract for the Chinese a security commitment from the Soviet Union, achieved only the latter aim; the shelling ceased in November. One unfortunate result of the Taiwan Strait crisis of 1958—and of the earlier similar crisis in 1955—was that tacit nuclear threats by the United States on nonnuclear China may have caused the Chinese to launch and accelerate their own nuclear-weapons program. The history of nuclear-weapons programs in such countries as China, India, Pakistan and perhaps even France suggests that nuclear threats against nonnuclear states strongly increase the incentives to acquire nuclear weapons.[4]

Just as the Taiwan Strait crisis cooled off, a new Berlin crisis was launched by the Soviets on November 27, when Moscow delivered a diplomatic note to the Western powers in Berlin. The note declared that the Soviet Union was dissatisfied with the "abnormal" status of the city of West Berlin, and proposed that its occupation by Western forces be terminated. If no agreement on transforming West Berlin into a free demilitarized city was forthcoming within six months, the note claimed, Moscow was prepared to turn over to the East Germans the rights to East Berlin and allow them to control all access routes to West Berlin.

Essentially, Moscow was attempting to force the Western powers either to recognize East Germany within six months or to withdraw from West Berlin. If they failed to do either, the note made clear, West Berlin would again be blockaded and efforts to break the blockade would mean war with the USSR.[5] In the event, however, after a series of conferences of foreign ministers, the Soviets backed away from the deadline but continued to press for Western recognition of East Germany.

In 1960, the long-smoldering Sino–Soviet conflict finally became public. The first issue openly raised by the Chinese was Khrushchev's ideological revisionism on the question of the inevitability of war with the capitalists. The Chinese thought Khrushchev was selling out by declaring that war could be avoided. In the famous April 1960 article in which the Chinese denounced Khrushchev, they asserted: "We believe in the absolute correctness of Lenin's thinking: War is an inevitable outcome of systems of exploitation and the source of modern wars is the imperialist system. Until the imperialist system and the exploiting classes come to an end, wars of one kind or another will always occur."[6] Mao had even told Khrushchev that the Chinese would welcome nuclear war, since no matter how it was fought, hundreds of millions of Chinese would survive.

One unfortunate result of the Sino–Soviet conflict was that Khrushchev was always wary of being too conciliatory to the West. Any Soviet move that appeared to reduce the chances of worldwide socialist revolution was loudly criticized by the Chinese as weak-willed and dangerous. Khrushchev's diplomacy, therefore, often appeared schizophrenic or duplicitous. The two main concerns of Soviet diplomacy, the United States and China, could not be addressed with consistent policies.

Only ten days after the Sino–Soviet rift was publicly exposed, Khrushchev was faced with another crisis, this time with the United States. On May 1, 1960, the Soviets finally succeeded in shooting down an American U-2 surveillance plane. U-2s had been overflying Soviet territory for years with complete impunity; the technology of Soviet air defenses was not sufficiently developed to shoot down the high-altitude spy plane. By 1960, however, the technology had been developed, and the plane, with pilot Francis Gary Powers, was shot out of the sky.

Khrushchev immediately declared that the Soviets had shot down the plane, but he did not disclose the fact that they had captured the pilot and his photographic equipment as well. Since U-2 pilots were instructed to destroy their planes at the first sign of trouble, and since U.S. experts doubted that a U-2 pilot could survive a shoot-down, the U.S. authorities, with no fear of contradiction, confidently claimed that the plane was conducting weather research. It was only then that Khrushchev revealed that the Soviets were holding the pilot and the evidence of the plane's spying capabilities. The U.S. State Department then admitted the full extent of U-2 surveillance of the Soviet Union, and, in an unprecedented move, publicly admitted that President Eisenhower had authorized the spying. Although Khrushchev may have hoped to embarrass the President and thereby prompt a more pliant U.S. attitude at the upcoming May summit, the President was not prepared to apologize for the U-2 mission, and the summit was aborted.

The Kennedy and Johnson Years

The next two years, the first years of the Kennedy Administration, witnessed several of the tensest episodes in the history of U.S.–Soviet relations. The tone of Soviet diplomacy toward the United States—a schizophrenic tone that combined hostility with offers to reduce tension—was set early on by Khrushchev. After the April 1961 Bay of Pigs operation, Khrushchev was both insulting and conciliatory toward President Kennedy. In a message to the President, he asserted that

61

"aggressive bandit acts cannot save your system," but he also added, "We wish to build up our relations with the United States in such a manner that the Soviet Union and the United States, as the two most powerful states in the world, would stop saber-rattling and bringing forward their military or economic advantage."[7]

The following month, on May 12, Khrushchev answered Kennedy's February message and agreed to a summit meeting in Vienna. At the meeting, which took place in June, it was fairly clear that Khrushchev's intent was to bully the new President. He revived the issue of West Berlin by threatening to sign a peace treaty with East Germany in December. Any Western agreement on access to the city, Khrushchev declared, would have to be negotiated with the East Germans.

Once again, Khrushchev, like Stalin, was probing to see if he could dislodge the Western powers from West Berlin by threatening to cut off their access to the city; if he could not dislodge them, he would probably have been satisfied with a series of treaties that confirmed the postwar borders in Europe. Khrushchev believed that the West would not offer significant resistance to a forceful Soviet effort.

The effort began when Soviet aircraft began to drop chaff (pieces of highly reflective metal) in the air corridors connecting Western Europe to West Berlin. Since this hindered the supplying of the city by air, NATO responded by increasing the number of ground convoys serving West Berlin; these ground convoys had to transit East German territory to reach the city. When the Soviets ordered the East Germans to stop and check the convoys, NATO guarded the convoys with military escorts fully prepared to use force to pass the border guards. Eventually, NATO forces came face to face with tanks of the Warsaw Pact, while Khrushchev was declaring that Soviet troops would mass on the West German border in the event of any serious developments.[8]

Meanwhile, three months after Khrushchev's original threat at the May summit, the symbol of the division of Berlin, the Berlin Wall, was erected on August 13. The Wall and other barriers along the East German border were designed to stop the hemorrhaging of East German citizens to the West; over three million had fled by the time of the construction of the Wall, many of them young adults, the most productive members of their society.

Soviet pressure was stepped up at the end of August 1961 when Moscow resumed the atmospheric testing of nuclear weapons, which it had suspended in 1958. Tests continued for two months and climaxed with the explosion of the largest nuclear device ever tested. Again, however, the Soviets retreated from their deadline in the face of U.S. resolve. At the Twenty-second Communist Party Congress in October, Khrushchev declared, "We shall not then insist on having a peace treaty definitely by December 31, 1961. The main thing is to decide the issue, to liquidate the remnants of war, to sign a peace treaty with Germany. That is the most important and essential problem."[9] Indeed, once Khrushchev became aware that the United States was not going to reduce its presence in Berlin, the most Khrushchev could hope for was a peace treaty that confirmed the status quo in Germany and in Europe as a whole.

The single most dangerous period in the postwar era began a year later, in October 1962. Soviet medium- and intermediate-range nuclear-tipped missiles were discovered in Cuba on October 15. On the 18th, the President held a long-scheduled meeting with Foreign Minister Gromyko, who said that Soviet activity in Cuba was not connected in any way with offensive operations against the United States. We knew this to be untrue. During the same period, the Soviet ambassador to the United States, Anatoliy Dobrynin, and the ambassador to the UN, Valerian Zorin, also claimed that there were no offensive missiles in Cuba. The public announcement of the discovery—accompanied by U-2 photos of the missile bases—and the imposition of a U.S. quarantine around Cuba came on October 22. The quarantine was designed to prevent further shipments of military hardware to Cuba.

The Soviet response of the following day was menacing: the Ministry of Defense placed its missile, bomber and submarine forces on alert and canceled all leaves. Warsaw Pact forces were also put on alert. Five days later, on Sunday morning, October 28, we received word that Moscow had agreed to remove the missiles, and within only a few hours crews were at work dismantling the missile sites.

The world has probably never been closer to the unleashing of nuclear catastrophe than it was during the thirteen days of the Cuban Missile Crisis. As I will emphasize later, the experience brought home to the leadership of both the United States and the Soviet Union the dangers implicit in the possession of nuclear weapons. Both nations therefore began to emphasize the importance of cooperation and mutual understanding in the cause of peace.

President Kennedy delivered a watershed speech in June 1963 at American University in Washington, D.C., in which he outlined the justification for his efforts to reduce tension with the Soviet Union. His words are equally appropriate for the situation today, over twenty-five years later:

> History teaches that enmities between nations, as between individuals, do not last forever. However fixed our likes and dislikes may seem, the tide of time and events will often bring surprising changes in the relations between nations and neighbors.
>
> . . . We are both devoting massive sums of money to weapons that could be better devoted to combating ignorance, poverty, and disease. We are both caught up in a vicious and dangerous cycle in which suspicion on one side breeds suspicion on the other and new weapons beget counterweapons . . . Agreements to this end [arms limitation] are in the interests of the Soviet Union as well as ours, and even the most hostile nations can be relied upon to accept and keep those treaty obligations, and only those treaty obligations, which are in their own interest.
>
> . . . We must, therefore, persevere in the search for

peace in the hope that constructive changes within the Communist bloc might bring within reach solutions which now seem beyond us. We must conduct our affairs in such a way that it becomes in the Communists' interest to agree on a genuine peace.[10]

Only six weeks after Kennedy's speech, on July 25, 1963, the United States, the Soviet Union and Great Britain signed the Limited Test Ban Treaty and agreed not to test nuclear weapons in the atmosphere, underwater or in space.

President Johnson continued Kennedy's efforts to strengthen the cooperative element of U.S.–Soviet relations. "We've got to get into the habit of peaceful cooperation," Johnson said in a statement to the Soviet people in September 1966. He emphasized the overriding common interest of the two countries in avoiding war and the record of friendly relations between the two peoples.[11] Among the cooperative ventures successfully launched in the Kennedy and Johnson years were the 1962 agreement on the neutralization of Laos, the 1963 creation of the permanent direct communication link between Moscow and Washington (the "hot line"), the treaty on peaceful uses of the Antarctic, and the nuclear nonproliferation treaty of 1968.

In addition, the Strategic Arms Limitation (SALT) process was initiated under President Johnson. In January of 1967, Johnson wrote to Soviet Prime Minister Alexey Kosygin suggesting bilateral talks on the limitation of strategic offensive and defensive systems. On

March 2, Johnson announced that Kosygin had answered his letter and had agreed to U.S.–Soviet discussions on the "means of limiting the arms race in offensive and defensive nuclear missiles." After several false starts, Soviet Foreign Minister Gromyko, in June 1968, signaled Soviet willingness to begin to negotiate. In a speech before the Supreme Soviet, Gromyko stated, "One of the unprobed areas of disarmament is the search for an understanding on mutual restriction and subsequent reduction of strategic vehicles for the delivery of nuclear weapons—offensive and defensive—including anti-missile. The Soviet Government is ready for an exchange of opinion on this subject."[12]

At the same time, during the spring and summer of 1968, the Czechoslovak people and their leadership were introducing a series of reforms into Czechoslovak political and social life. Their attempts to institute "socialism with a human face" in Czechoslovakia ultimately proved unacceptable to the Soviet leadership; the internal liberalization and foreign-policy autonomy developing in Czechoslovakia threatened "stability" not only in that country but in other East European states as well. On the night of August 20, Soviet tanks rolled into Czechoslovakia, putting an end to reform in that country and forcing the United States to shelve plans for negotiating with the Soviets on strategic arms. The invasion also sparked the growth of "Eurocommunism" in 1968. For the first time, West European Communist parties were distancing themselves from Moscow's policies and condemning Soviet actions.

In the second half of the 1960s, although Presidents Kennedy and Johnson had attempted to broaden and strengthen U.S.–Soviet cooperative efforts, Soviet interest in such cooperation dwindled as the American presence in Vietnam grew.

The cause for the Soviet shift was not necessarily a genuine perception that American involvement in Vietnam either threatened Soviet security or prevented further efforts toward cooperation. Vietnam, of course, confirmed Moscow's assumption that U.S. and Soviet security interests were at odds with each other. But Moscow often proves itself willing to overlook differences and conflicts when it is in Soviet interests to do so. (The Soviets went ahead with the 1972 summit, and the signing of the SALT I accords, for example, only one month after the U.S. bombing of Haiphong harbor had accidentally damaged four Soviet merchant ships, with loss of Soviet lives.) It was, therefore, not primarily the security implications of Vietnam that provoked Soviet leaders to reduce cooperation with the United States. Rather, Moscow was quick to take advantage of the propaganda value of American involvement in Vietnam.

Soviet propagandists presented a simple alternative to those peoples and leaders of the Third World that were seeking assistance from larger powers. The Soviet Union in January of 1966 in Tashkent had served as host and chief intermediary for the peace talks that settled the five-month-long Indo–Pakistani war of 1965. As a result of the Tashkent talks, the Soviet Union appeared to many Third World nations to be a better guarantor of their interests than either China or the United States.

The Soviets managed to extract a great deal of propaganda mileage out of the Vietnam War. In addition, the Soviet image on the world scene benefited from the introversion of both the United States and China. The United States was, of course, involved in Vietnam and deeply concerned about the domestic troubles that accompanied that involvement, and China was preoccupied entirely by its Cultural Revolution, a deep and violent overhaul of the Chinese political and social systems, accompanied by massive purges, dislocations and upheavals. The Soviet Union no longer seemed like the superpower that represented the threat of war; its image abroad, in spite of the invasion of Czechoslovakia, was a peaceful and businesslike one.

The Era of Détente

Partly as a result of this new image, and partly as a result of the goals of the new leadership in Washington and Bonn, the Soviets entered the 1970s as the cooperative partner with the United States and Western Europe in what would soon be known as "détente." Détente with the Soviet Union was, in a sense, introduced by West Germany as a result of Bonn's signing of "peace" treaties with the Soviet Union (1970), Poland (1970) and East Germany (1972). These treaties and the four-power agreement on Berlin (1971) confirmed the postwar European boundaries and the East and West European status quo. Much of what Khrushchev had vigorously pressed for in the Berlin crises of 1958–59 and 1960–61 was finally achieved by his successor.

Following closely on the heels of Soviet–West European détente was détente with the United States. Richard M. Nixon announced in his inaugural speech in January 1969 that he hoped to open an "era of negotiation" with the Soviet Union, and the Soviets were eager to respond. According to Harry Gelman, the Soviets sought to achieve at least three goals in détente. First and foremost, they hoped to strengthen themselves against the perceived foreign-policy threat from the People's Republic of China (PRC) and sought to enlist U.S. cooperation in their struggles against the Chinese. Second, the Soviet economy desperately needed an infusion of Western, especially American, technology. Third, they sought to place constraints on the increasingly expensive strategic-arms race with the United States.[13]

The goals of Nixon and Secretary of State Henry A. Kissinger overlapped with those of the Soviet Union only on the issue of SALT. The primary goal of the United States was to encourage Soviet support of, or at least passive acquiescence in, the U.S. efforts to extract American troops from Vietnam. According to Raymond Garthoff, a senior officer in the State Department, "The dominant foreign policy preoccupation of Nixon and Kissinger in 1969, and indeed for the entire period through 1972, was not a detente summit meeting with

Moscow, but finding an honorable exit from Vietnam."[14] Kissinger himself has written that he hoped in 1969 "to enlist the Soviet Union in a rapid settlement of the Vietnam war. In all my conversations with Dobrynin I had stressed that a fundamental improvement in U.S.– Soviet relations presupposed Soviet cooperation in settling the war."[15]

An additional goal which Nixon and Kissinger sought to achieve was the creation of a "network of relations" that would restrain Soviet behavior.[16] Nixon and Kissinger referred to this network as a "structure of peace." They hoped that by intensifying the involvement of the Soviet Union in the day-to-day politics and economics of an increasingly interdependent world, Soviet incentives to disrupt the workings of the international system would sharply decline.

Détente was never very clearly thought through on the U.S. side, however, in Garthoff's view. As late as 1972, he argues, U.S. policy toward the Soviet Union was largely ad hoc; as evidence, he cites Nixon's readiness in 1972 to forgo the Moscow summit if that proved to be the cost of the intensified bombing of North Vietnam.[17] Détente was justified in part by the need to moderate Soviet behavior in an era when the United States was choosing to decrease the extent of its security commitments abroad. In the early months of his first term, the President promulgated the "Nixon Doctrine," which held that dispatch of U.S. troops abroad was likely to become increasingly rare. Nixon guaranteed continued nuclear deterrence of aggression against

U.S. allies and other key states, but "in cases involving other types of aggression . . . we shall look to the nation directly threatened to assume the primary responsibility of providing the manpower for its defense."[18] Retracting American commitments in this manner, Nixon recognized the necessity of attempts to secure guarantees regarding Soviet behavior in the Third World.

In the view of the Soviet leadership, on the other hand, détente was made possible by the recent increase in Soviet military power, in particular the attainment of a nuclear retaliatory capability in the early 1960s and, more important, the clear achievement of strategic parity by the late 1960s or early 1970s.[19] Military parity forced the United States to treat the Soviet Union as an equal. Interestingly, Soviet analysts do not suggest that parity requires exact equality of weapons arsenals. Parity is guaranteed merely by the ability of both powers to destroy each other in a retaliatory strike: "Parity does not mean absolute equality of available means. It means that we can mutually destroy each other with sufficient certainty."[20]

The Soviets never believed that détente should affect either Soviet domestic policy or Soviet support for revolutionary and socialist regimes abroad. In the words of George Kennan:

> The Soviet leaders were determined that the development should not affect the intactness of the dictatorship at home; nor was it to hinder them from continuing to adopt, with relation to the problems of third countries,

a rhetorical and political stance of principled revolutionary Marxism, designed to protect them from charges by Chinese Communists that they were betraying the cause of Marxism-Leninism.[21]

Leonid Brezhnev himself declared at the Twenty-fifth Communist Party Congress, "Détente does not in the slightest way abolish, and cannot abolish or change, the laws of the class struggle. We do not conceal the fact that we see détente as a way to create more favorable conditions for peaceful socialist and Communist construction."[22] The Soviets were declaring themselves free to support any "national liberation" or revolutionary movement that they cared to.

Despite the differing Soviet and American conceptions of the causes and purposes of détente, the two superpowers made several important achievements during détente's short tenure. The most significant by far was the signing at the May 1972 summit of the Anti–Ballistic Missile (ABM) Treaty. The ABM Treaty almost completely closed off competition in antimissile systems, and thereby reduced incentives for offensive buildups. A world in which strategic-defense technology was unconstrained would witness fierce and costly arms races in both offensive and defensive systems.

Another achievement was the signing of the SALT I Agreement itself, which limited construction of launchers of offensive missile systems, causing the Soviet Union to level off its production of ICBMs and probably prompting the Soviets to retire some older

ICBM systems that they might otherwise have maintained. The SALT I Agreement also created the Standing Consultative Commission, a forum in which the United States and the Soviet Union can air grievances about compliance or other arms-control issues.

There is little question, however, that détente could have achieved more. For example, analysts agree that the opportunity to limit or ban MIRVs (multiple independently targetable reentry vehicles) in 1972 should not have been allowed to slip away. U.S. negotiators did not wish to limit MIRVs, because of the U.S. lead in MIRV technology. It was only a matter of time, however, before the Soviets caught up and threatened U.S. systems with MIRVs of their own. In 1974 Henry Kissinger admitted, "I would say in retrospect that I wish I had thought through the implications of a MIRVed world more thoughtfully in 1969 and in 1970 than I did."[23]

In addition, the Basic Principles Agreement, signed by Nixon and Brezhnev in 1972, could have been designed as an important document offering guidelines for U.S. and Soviet behavior in the Third World and elsewhere. In reality, however, it is full of generalities and was never regarded as a serious guide to behavior by either side.

As the Nixon presidency disintegrated in 1973 and 1974 as a result of disclosures about the Watergate scandal, anti-détente forces "moved again to the battle lines, and with great effectiveness."[24] Senator Henry "Scoop" Jackson of Washington co-sponsored an amendment to the Trade Bill of 1974 which prevented the President from extending most-favored-nation treatment to the Soviet Union and prohibited the U.S. Export-Import Bank from financing U.S.–Soviet transactions as long as the Soviet Union denied its citizens the right to free emigration. As a result, not only were U.S.–Soviet economic relations stillborn; Soviet emigration figures plummeted as well in response to U.S. interference in Soviet domestic affairs. In Kennan's words, "The Jackson-Vanik amendment, and the subsequent demise of the trade pact, dealt a bitter blow to any hopes for retaining the very considerable momentum that had been obtained in the development of Soviet–American relations."[25]

Later that same year, the December 1974 passage of the Stevenson Amendment to the Export-Import Bank Bill limited the amount the bank could guarantee in loans to the USSR to $300 million over the following four years. Higher amounts required congressional approval, and none of the money could be used for the production of energy. The Soviet Union had hoped for sizable U.S. loans to assist in its massive Yakutsk/North Star Siberian energy projects. Gelman may have overstated the case when he wrote that "these capital transfers and the associated technology inputs were probably the biggest single dividend the Politburo had anticipated from the detente relationship,"[26] but the Soviets were without question deeply disappointed and very suspicious after the passage of the Jackson-Vanik and Stevenson amendments.

By the end of 1974, disillusionment about détente

had taken root both in Washington and in Moscow. The Soviets found that (1) the U.S. was not willing to transfer capital and technology on the scale that Moscow desired; (2) the U.S. was not willing to side with the USSR against China; (3) the U.S. was more willing to intrude in Soviet internal matters; and (4) the U.S. was reacting negatively to Soviet international efforts to expand influence and power. On the American side, Washington was disappointed that (1) the Soviets had proved unwilling to cease aiding Hanoi; (2) Moscow was proceeding with new modifications of strategic nuclear weapon systems (introducing a fourth generation of ICBMs, for example); (3) deployment of Soviet SS-20s in the European portion of Russia increased Moscow's nuclear superiority in Europe; and (4) Moscow had shown little restraint in encouraging pro-Soviet changes in the Third World.[27]

Apart from these specific grievances, Raymond Garthoff has pointed to five more general reasons why détente failed to take firm root in U.S.–Soviet relations:[28]

1. Above all, Washington and Moscow entered détente with drastically different conceptions of its causes and implications. The United States wanted to manage Soviet international activity, while the Soviets viewed détente as a way to manage the transition of the United States from superiority to parity.

2. The two sides failed to turn to "collaborative measures" to ensure national and global security.

National military power, in Garthoff's view, is vital to national security, but "it need not be the first, or usual, or sole, recourse."

3. The United States and the Soviet Union failed to define a meaningful code of conduct, one that could actually guide behavior in tense circumstances.

4. Each side thought the other was developing its military capabilities in a manner incompatible with détente.

5. Neither side realized how détente interacted with the domestic politics of the other. The United States tried to interfere in Soviet domestic affairs, and the Soviets never fully understood the difficulties that can arise between the executive and legislative branches of the U.S. system.

Soviet leaders were also wrong when they judged that the passivity of U.S. foreign policy would be long-lived. The Nixon Doctrine was not destined to be a permanent reflection of U.S. foreign-policy attitudes, and when U.S. global activism rose to its traditional postwar level, the Soviets thought that Washington was reneging on an implicit bargain.

Soviet Expansionist Activity in the Late 1970s

One of the most troublesome features of the détente era, from the U.S. point of view, was the surge in Soviet activism in the Third World after 1975. While such great-power expansionism probably could have been foreseen, it was poorly understood and was interpreted as illegitimate by successive American administrations.

In the mid-1950s, Khrushchev courted the "national bourgeoisie" in such countries as Nehru's India, Nasser's Egypt, Sukarno's Indonesia and Ben-Bella's Algeria. Khrushchev devoted Soviet attention to these regimes because they appeared receptive to anti-Western blandishments and because the local Communist parties were simply too weak to represent a reliable means of influence. He praised these leaders as "national democrats" who were paving the way for "socialist revolutions." The Soviets advised Communists in these countries to cooperate with the national democrats, even if they had to dissolve their party organizations.[29]

The results of this strategy were very disappointing. Nasser's successor, Anwar Sadat, expelled the Soviets in the early 1970s. Sukarno, Ben-Bella and Ghana's President Kwame Nkrumah were ousted in military coups. In other countries, Communists were jailed or executed, and in none of these states was the Soviet foreign-policy line wholly adopted.

The Soviet reaction to the failures of the 1950s and 1960s was to abandon the policy of supporting "national democrats" and to begin to aid Marxist-Leninist parties in the Third World. It was agreed that the "national democrats" were unreliable partners and that only fellow Marxist-Leninists should, with certain exceptions, serve as the primary defenders of Soviet interests abroad. Once the Soviets achieved the material capability to aid such parties, and once Soviet equality with the United States was codified in détente, Moscow launched a policy of Third World activism that took many in the West by surprise.

Between 1975 and 1979, seven pro-Soviet Communist parties seized power or territory in Asia and Africa:

In the spring of 1975, North Vietnamese troops took control of South Vietnam.

At the same time, the Pathet Lao, clients of the North Vietnamese, took power in Laos.

In the Angolan Civil War of 1975–76, Agostinho Neto's Popular Movement for the Liberation of Angola (MPLA) defeated all other contenders for power.

In February 1977, Colonel Mengistu Haile Mariam seized power in Ethiopia.

In April 1978, Nur Mohammed Taraki's People's Party seized power in an armed coup in Afghanistan.

In June 1978, the Communists in the ruling coalition of South Yemen carried out a successful armed coup against the non-Communists.

In January 1979, the North Vietnamese invaded Cambodia and replaced the Pol Pot government with a pro-Soviet regime.[30]

The Soviets were not, by any means, wholly responsible for any of these developments. But in each instance they were actively involved. In the case of

Angola, for example, the Soviets airlifted to the scene of the conflict Soviet arms and 10,000 Cuban troops. In Ethiopia, the Soviets again provided an airlift, this time delivering over $2 billion worth of arms, 20,000 Cuban troops, 300 tanks and 3,000 Soviet military technicians.[31]

Soviet activity in Africa and Asia in the late 1970s can be explained quite simply. The Soviets believed that they had finally reached political and military equality with the United States; they therefore felt entitled to undertake such moves. They were also materially capable of the actions. Moreover, the paralyzed presidency of the post-Watergate years and the relatively passive response of the Carter Administration to early Soviet moves persuaded the Soviets that the Third World presented opportunities that could be exploited at relatively low cost and risk.

In addition to Asia and Africa, Moscow's growing confidence in its power was exhibited in another region as well, the Middle East. In the 1956 and 1967 Arab–Israeli wars, Moscow's role was minimal, and Soviet influence on the outcome was nonexistent. During the 1970 war, however, the USSR delivered advanced aircraft and missiles to Egypt, and the Soviet troop presence there reached a high of twenty thousand. In 1973, Soviet behavior was menacing as well. In April, Moscow issued a joint statement with Egypt declaring that if occupied Arab territory was not peacefully surrendered by Israel it could be recovered by force. During the October War itself, Moscow undertook a massive resupply of the Arab effort, proposed a joint U.S.–Soviet effort to maintain the subsequent cease-fire, and delivered a well-known statement to President Nixon asserting that if the United States did not cooperate, the Soviet Union might find it necessary to act alone. In view of the possibility of unilaterial Soviet action in the Middle East, the U.S. Strategic Air Command and the North American Defense Command were placed on alert. The alert lasted approximately two days, and the situation was finally defused only by the United States's pressing Israel to accept the terms of the cease-fire.

The Carter Years

The Carter Administration entered office near the height of Soviet international confidence. Its critics maintain that it failed to present a consistent image or a coherent set of policies to the Soviet Union. Raymond Garthoff states that "especially at the outset, President Carter often acted intuitively on his own, and even later he moved in different directions as events led him to turn to different advisers. The result was a policy that zigzagged."[32] In William Taubman's view, "Understanding Carter's zig-zags was a challenge for even the most dispassionate observer. For the Soviets it proved an impossible assignment."[33]

The leadership in Moscow expressed a number of grievances: Carter's 1977 shift on the U.S. SALT II position; his outspokenness on human rights; his switching from inviting the Soviets to participate in the

Middle East peace process to excluding them; the speed with which relations with the People's Republic of China were normalized; and the U.S. protests regarding the presence of Soviet troops in Cuba.

After the coups in Ethiopia, South Yemen and Afghanistan, President Carter forcefully denounced the Soviet view of détente. At a June 1978 speech in Annapolis, Carter condemned Soviet Third World activism and introduced the hard line that was to characterize the remaining years of his presidency. "To the Soviet Union," he stated, "détente seems to mean a continuing aggressive struggle for political advantage and increased influence in a variety of ways. A competition without restraint and without shared rules will escalate into graver tensions and our relationship as a whole will suffer."[34]

The Soviet invasion of Afghanistan in December 1979 was motivated not by a perceived weakness in Washington, but by the Soviets' own evaluation of their security requirements. An extremely hard line emanating from Washington may have prolonged the Soviet assessment of the costs and benefits of the invasion, but the United States probably could not have prevented the Soviet attack. As a response to the Soviet incursion, the Carter Administration postponed the Senate vote on the ratification of the SALT II Treaty, blocked $2 billion in grain sales to the USSR, prevented American athletes from participating in the 1980 Moscow Olympics, halted sales of advanced technology to the Soviet Union, increased military aid to Pakistan after earlier refusing to do so, and accelerated contacts with the People's Republic of China. U.S.–Soviet relations never recovered from the effects of Afghanistan until the tenure in Moscow of Mikhail Gorbachev.

By the time of the Afghanistan invasion, the Soviets had also drawn up a long list of grievances regarding U.S. international behavior. The United States had punished Moscow for its invasion of Afghanistan, for example, but had taken no action whatsoever in response to the Chinese intervention in Vietnam only months before. In fact, the United States appeared to have encouraged China to launch the invasion and to intensify its arming of the Cambodian forces of Pol Pot. At the same time, the U.S. was coordinating opposition activity in Afghanistan, Nicaragua and Poland, and seemed to have arranged the "defection" of Sadat's Egypt, the Sudan, and Somalia from the Soviet camp. The United States successfully deprived the Soviet Union of a role in the Middle East peace process after repeated promises that it had no intention of doing so. And Washington assisted in the overthrow of an elected Marxist, Salvador Allende, in Chile.[35]

The 1980s

But airing these grievances was to do Moscow no good. By the 1980s, Soviet foreign policy was causing enormous problems for itself by emphasizing the military over any other policy instruments. The Soviet strategic buildup, the deployment of SS-20s in Europe and the massing of troops and military hardware in Asia were doing Moscow more harm than good. The strategic buildup gave rise to the increased defense budgets of the Reagan presidency, totaling over two trillion dollars in eight years. The SS-20s in Europe, similarly, provoked the December 1979 NATO decision to modernize Western intermediate-range nuclear forces, and Soviet troops and SS-20s in Asia led to heightened Chinese security cooperation with the United States, and improved U.S.–Japanese ties as well.

Partly as a result of the militarization of Soviet foreign policy, and partly as a result of domestic American developments, U.S.–Soviet relations fell to a dangerous low during the first years of the Reagan presidency. The stridency of the Reagan view of the Soviet Union, combined with the ailing Soviet leadership's inability to address any of its problems in a creative or original fashion, prohibited the development of any efforts to construct a cooperative U.S.–Soviet relationship.

In his first White House news conference, on January 29, 1981, President Reagan charged—in a simplistic misreading of Soviet ideology—that the leaders of the Soviet Union "reserve unto themselves the right to commit any crime, to lie, to cheat" in order to further their cause.[36] In March 1983, only weeks before he delivered his famous "Star Wars" speech, Reagan called the Soviet Union "the focus of evil in the modern world."[37] At the same time, the Soviet leadership was comparing the United States to Nazi Germany, an analogy that the Soviets, having lost twenty million citizens to the Nazis in World War II, do not take lightly.

The lowest point in the relationship came on September 1, 1983, when the Soviet Union shot down Korean Air Lines Flight 007, killing all 269 people aboard. The plane had evidently strayed accidentally into Soviet airspace, and after tracking it for several hours Soviet Air Defense forces destroyed it. Because of the hostile nature of the relationship, each side immediately charged the other with complete disregard for the lives of the passengers. The Soviets claimed that the United States had cynically involved innocent lives in an espionage mission, and Washington charged—on the basis of insufficient evidence, as it turned out—that the Soviets had been aware that the plane was a civilian airliner.

At the end of the month, in an unusual statement issued in his capacity as chief of party and state, Yuri Andropov declared that the United States was on "a militarist course that represents a serious threat to peace. Its essence is to attempt to ensure a dominant position in the world for the United States of America without regard for the interests of other states and peoples." Andropov argued that "if anyone had any illusions about the possibility of an evolution for the better in the policy of the present American administration, recent events have dispelled them once and for all."[38] In other words, Andropov was completely writing off the Reagan Administration. The infirm leadership of Konstantin Chernenko continued that approach into 1985.

Before turning to the policy changes following the rise to power of Mikhail Gorbachev in 1985, I will explore, in the next section, the costs of the Cold War to the participants.

III

The Costs of the Conflict

The four decades of conflict outlined in Chapters I and II have been immensely costly to both sides. As I stated in the Introduction, for the United States they have led to huge defense expenditures, $2.4 trillion over the past eight years, turned our attention away from urgent domestic problems, distorted our relations with other nations and moved us away from our traditional values. The costs for the Soviet Union have been at least as great. And the continuing series of political crises which have marked the postwar years have carried the risk of escalation into military confrontation which would endanger the survival of both of our societies. In this chapter I will elaborate on these points.

The Financial and Economic Costs

No work of nonficton has received more attention in recent months than Paul Kennedy's book *The Rise and Fall of the Great Powers*. In it he examines the changing relationships among nations over a period of five hundred years. Based on that analysis, he concludes that when the security commitments and economic strength of Great Powers move out of balance they fall into decline. The implication is that the United States and the Soviet Union are at such a point today. I question whether such a conclusion applies to the United States, but it almost certainly does to the Soviet Union.

Kennedy's book followed by a few months an article in *The Economist* entitled "Has America Lost Its Smile?" It suggested that the United States, on which the postwar world had depended for leadership in both economic and political affairs, had lost its sense of compassion, its optimism and its self-confidence. As a result, said *The Economist*, we had withdrawn from our leadership role, we had turned inward, and because of our pessimistic mood, we had even lost our ability to deal with our own domestic problems. I agree with that appraisal. But I believe that our failure to move toward a solution of both our domestic and our international problems is more a function of our psychological strength and our political will than our economic capacity. And I see no evidence whatsoever to support the conclusion that our problem is a function of an imbalance between our economic capacity and our security commitments. We should not forget that more than thirty-five years ago, when real income per capita in the United States was less than half what it is today, we launched the Marshall Plan; in terms of the share of gross national product, we contributed more than ten times as much to development assistance as we do now and at the same time diverted to defense a significantly higher percentage of our GNP than at present.

Our financial problem today is not that we cannot afford financially to fight the Cold War, but rather that we have grossly mismanaged our program for doing so. We have spent far more than was necessary on defense. We have refused to increase taxes to pay for the rising expenditures. The necessary funds to finance the deficit have been raised by borrowing from abroad, thereby burdening future generations. And to minimize the foreign borrowing, we have shortchanged nondefense expenditures. As a result, severe economic and social problems plague our society.

The indiscriminate priority given to defense expenditures has led to waste on an enormous scale. In 1983, Cyrus Vance, McGeorge Bundy, Admiral Elmo Zumwalt and I—as former Secretaries of State and Defense, former National Security Adviser and retired Chief of Naval Operations—were asked by the Congress for our views on the defense program proposed by President Reagan for the fiscal years 1984–88. I quote from our reply:

In total, for the five-year period 1984–1988, we believe the increase in cash outlays for defense can be cut $136 billion below the level proposed by the Administration.

In advocating these reductions in the President's proposals, we wish to emphasize strong agreement with him on two points:

1. The primary duty of any President is the defense of this nation; and
2. This nation can afford whatever is necessary to maintain that defense.

We recognize, as well, that the Soviet Union, whatever its motives, has been investing large and increasing resources in its armed forces. In our view, the Soviet Union does not wish large scale war with the West. But it is likely that in the future, as in the past, it will probe for weakness and take advantage of it wherever it can find it.

In such a world, it would be folly for the United States to underfund its defense needs, especially when the resources of this country exceed those of prospective adversaries by a substantial amount. It would be equally reckless to employ those resources indiscriminately for defense, especially when there are other vital uses for them and when the United States has no interest in spurring the arms race. Admittedly, the line between the two is difficult to walk. Even defining the line is an imperfect art. We are nonetheless convinced that the United States has strayed far from that line, and strayed in the direction of doing too much rather than too little. We are convinced we can have equal military strength and greater economic strength—with lower defense expenditures.

But the cuts which we recommended were not made. For the eight-year period 1981–88, defense expenditures totaled approximately $2.4 trillion. Two former Secretaries of Defense agreed recently that equivalent security could have been procured for $200 to $250 billion less.

The situation in the Soviet Union is quite different from that in the United States. And there, as I said earlier, Paul Kennedy's thesis may indeed be applicable.

The economic crisis in the Soviet Union is far more severe than many of us in the West have recognized. The GNP growth rate, estimated at 6 percent per annum in the 1960s, 4 percent per annum in the '70s, and 2 percent per annum in the early '80s, has been stagnant for the past several years.

The effects of the stagnant economy have been reflected in basic measures of social welfare: life expectancy has fallen, infant mortality has risen, and alcoholism has increased.

Gorbachev, in *Perestroika,* spoke of a society in crisis. He recognized that it would be difficult, if not impossible, to finance the investment required to expand productivity and make the Soviet Union into a strong competitor in the global market in the twenty-first century, without reducing the inordinately high level of defense expenditures.

In contrast to the 6 percent of GNP which we devote to defense, the CIA estimates that the Soviets are spending a minimum of 17 percent. They do appear to be an example of a Great Power in which economic strength and security commitments are out of balance. If their economy is to be strengthened and prepared for the twenty-first century, defense outlays, in relation to GNP, must be reduced. Gorbachev clearly hopes to move in that direction. His recognition of the need to do so and his wish to accomplish that objective without endangering security is, I believe, a major factor causing him to reappraise Soviet foreign policy.

The price of the Cold War has been high not just to the United States and the Soviet Union and their allies, but to the rest of the world—the South—as well. Since 1945, wars claiming an estimated eighteen million, mostly civilian, casualties have been fought in the developing countries with weapons provided by the industrialized and socialist worlds. In March of 1988 alone there were twenty-five wars going on in the world, all in the Third World and all fought with weapons from the First and Second Worlds. Four-fifths of the over three million casualties in these wars have been civilians.[1]

These conflicts are, in most cases, a reflection of age-old religious, ethnic and political differences. But they have been fueled by Great Power rivalry, and the mechanism to resolve the disputes before they degenerate into military conflict—the collective-security system of the United Nations—has been rendered impotent by Great Power design.

The Distortion of Values

The overriding priority which we in the United States gave to actions designed to counter what we viewed as Soviet aggression has distorted our values both in economic and social affairs and in foreign policy. And the emphasis in the Soviet Union on preparing for and sustaining the Cold War appears to have had the same effect there as well.

In the United States, the effect was not limited to excessive and wasteful defense expenditures, but, more important, we were blinded to the actions required to effectively address many of our most serious domestic problems. We are facing, therefore, unacceptably high levels of unemployment, particularly among blacks and teenagers; a rapidly growing "underclass"—51 percent of the births in the capital of the richest nation in the world, Washington, D.C., are illegitimate; high and rising rates of drug abuse and drug-related crime; a failure to adequately address the problems of the poor and disadvantaged; a deterioriating physical infrastructure; severe distortion in sectoral and regional growth patterns; and irresponsible economic policies toward other nations in both the developed and the developing worlds.

One of the great achievements of the American political and social structure is our ability to maintain political cohesiveness in a society as ethnically diverse as ours. This stability depends on preserving a reasonable degree of economic equity among the various social groups. Recent government policies toward minorities

95

and the economically disadvantaged have been jeopardizing the preservation of that equity.[2]

The distortion of our values has not been limited to economic and social affairs. It has affected foreign policy as well. Throughout our history we have viewed our nation as the defender of freedom and democracy throughout the world. But in recent decades, on occasion after occasion, when confronted with a choice between support of democratic governments and support of anti-Soviet dictatorships, we have turned our back on our traditional values and have supported the antidemocratic regimes. That has been particularly true of our interventions in Latin America, but we have also backed authoritarian regimes in Zaire, the Philippines, Iran and elsewhere. If the United States stands for the defense of freedom both at home and abroad, our support of repressive regimes is a tragedy.

The Risk of Destruction Through Nuclear War[3]

Along with the economic and social costs, the Cold War has brought the risk of destruction of our society through nuclear war. We rarely discuss this subject. I will try to put it in perspective by summarizing the evolution of U.S. and Soviet nuclear forces and by reporting a personal experience relating to the possible use of the weapons.

Nearly fifty years have passed since Albert Einstein sent his historic letter to President Roosevelt warning him that it was essential that the United States move quickly to develop the nuclear bomb. In that half century the world's inventory of such weapons has increased from zero to fifty thousand. On average, each of them has a destructive power approximately thirty times that of the Hiroshima bomb. A few hundred could destroy not only the nations of NATO and the Warsaw Pact, but, through atmospheric effects, a major part of the rest of the world as well.

The weapons are widely deployed. They are supported by war-fighting strategies. Detailed war plans for their use are in the hands of the field commanders. And the troops of each side routinely undertake exercises specifically designed to prepare for that use. General Bernard Rogers, the retired Supreme Allied Commander of NATO forces in Europe, has said it was likely that in the early hours or early days of a military conflict in Western Europe, he would in fact have asked for the authority to initiate such use.

This situation has evolved over the years through a series of incremental decisions. I myself participated in many of them. Each of the decisions, taken by itself, appeared rational or inescapable. But the fact is that they were made without reference to any overall master plan or long-term objective. They have led to nuclear arsenals and nuclear war plans that few of the participants either anticipated or would, in retrospect, wish to support.

In the tense atmosphere of a crisis, each side will feel pressure to delegate authority to fire nuclear weapons to battlefield commanders. As the likelihood of attack increases, these commanders will face a desperate dilemma: use them or lose them. And because the strategic nuclear forces, and the complex systems designed to command them, are perceived by many to be vulnerable to a preemptive attack, they will argue the advantage of a preemptive strike.

But it is a fact that in the face of the opponent's nuclear forces, neither side has found it possible to develop plans for the use of its nuclear weapons in ways that would avoid the very high risk of escalating to all-out nuclear war.

What would be the consequences of such a conflict?

Studies by the Defense Department have concluded that even under the most favorable assumptions, there is a high risk of 100 million dead in the United States and Western Europe alone.

Studies such as these have prompted Helmut Schmidt, the former Chancellor of the Federal Republic of Germany, to state that the use of nuclear weapons will not defend the West, but destroy it.[4]

Field Marshal Lord Carver, Lord Louis Mountbatten and several other of the eight retired chiefs of the British Defense Staff share Schmidt's views.[5]

It is true that four decades have passed without the use of nuclear weapons, and it is clear that both NATO and the Warsaw Pact are aware of the dangers of nuclear war. As I have said, I do not believe the Soviet Union wants war with the West. And certainly the West will not attack the USSR or its allies. But dangerous

98

frictions between East and West have developed in the past and are likely to do so in the future. If deterrence fails and conflict develops, the present strategy of both NATO and the Warsaw Pact carries with it a high risk that civilization will be destroyed.

The Soviets have studied the origin and implications of the East–West confrontations over the past three decades, in particular those relating to Berlin, Cuba and the Middle East. They have recognized, perhaps even more than do the political leaders in the West, the great danger that through misinformation, misjudgment and miscalculation such crises may escalate. Their sensitivity to such risks was evident at a meeting I attended in Moscow in January 1989.

The Soviet government, in association with Harvard University, invited McGeorge Bundy and Theodore Sorensen, two close associates of President Kennedy, and me to join four Soviet officials (former Foreign Minister Andrey Gromyko, former Ambassador to the U.S. Anatoliy Dobrynin, Fyodor Burlatsky, Khrushchev's personal assistant, and Georgi Shaknazarov, a senior staff member of the Central Committee, as well as three Cuban officials who are close associates of Fidel Castro (Messrs. Risket Valdés, Aragone Navarro and Del Valle Jiménez) to discuss the causes of the Cuban Missile Crisis and the lessons to be learned from that event.

In 1962, the Soviet Union, under the cloak of secrecy, and with the clear intent to deceive, had introduced intermediate-range nuclear missiles into Cuba. A series of actions followed which brought the United States and the Soviet Union to the verge of military conflict and the world to the brink of nuclear disaster.

At the Moscow meeting, the Soviets with extraordinary candor indicated that Khrushchev had acted in a spirit of adventurism and without consideration of the consequences. But, more fundamentally, Khrushchev did what he did, and Kennedy responded as he did, because each leader, his associates and his people were captives of the gross misperceptions and deep-seated mistrust which underlay the Cold War—misperceptions and mistrust that exist to this day.

In addition, it is now clear that the decisions before and during the crisis were distorted as well by misinformation and miscalculation:

Before the Soviet missiles were introduced into Cuba in the summer of 1962, the Soviets and the Cubans believed that the United States intended to invade the island to overthrow Castro and his government. But I can say without qualification that we had no such intention.

The United States believed that the Soviets would not move nuclear warheads outside the Soviet Union. They did. In Moscow, we were told that by October 24 twenty Soviet warheads had been delivered to Cuba and that their missiles were targeted on U.S. cities.

The Soviets believed that the missiles could be introduced secretly into Cuba, without detection, and when their presence was disclosed the United

States would not respond. Here too they were in error.

Finally, those who urged President Kennedy to destroy the missiles by a U.S. air attack, to be followed in all probability by a sea and land invasion, were almost certainly mistaken in their belief that the Soviets would not respond with military action. At the time, the CIA had reported 10,000 Soviet troops in Cuba. We learned in Moscow that there were 40,000. We know now, too, that there were 270,000 well-armed Cuban troops. Both forces were determined, in the words of their commanders, to "fight to the death." The Cuban officials estimated they would have suffered 100,000 casualties. The Soviets expressed disbelief we would have thought that, in the face of such a catastrophic defeat, they would not have responded militarily somewhere in the world, most likely against U.S. Jupiter missiles in Turkey or NATO forces in Berlin.

By Saturday, October 27, 1962, the crisis had reached such a point that Burlatsky told us he and a Central Committee colleague decided to move their wives and children to the countryside in anticipation of a U.S. nuclear strike on Moscow. And, at the same time in Washington, on a beautiful fall evening, as I left the President's office to return to the Pentagon, I thought I might never live to see another Saturday night. I know this sounds melodramatic, but it reflects the state of mind of the participants on both sides at that critical moment in the crisis.

What were the lessons learned?

We agreed there were two: (1) In this nuclear age, crisis management is dangerous, difficult, uncertain; it is not possible to predict with confidence the consequences of military action between the superpowers and their allies because of misjudgment, misinformation, miscalculation. (2) Therefore, we must direct our attention to crisis avoidance—and that means reducing political tensions between East and West and striking at the misperceptions and mistrust that underlie such tensions.

In the twenty-six years that have passed since the Missile Crisis, we have made little progress in that direction. In the pages which follow I will explore the extent to which major steps can be taken to shrink dramatically the basis for East–West conflict. But before doing so, I wish to examine one additional "cost" of the Cold War: the moral implications of our policies.

The Moral Dimension of the East–West Nuclear Confrontation

Most human beings are basically moral. We understand that our behavior—our individual behavior and our national behavior—does affect other individuals and other nations, and we recognize that we have a responsibility to behave in ways consistent with the basic rights of others. And yet, all too often we fail to bring the moral dimension into discussions of national and international issues. My experience has been that one is thought to be naive if he introduces such considerations into public-policy debates, particularly debates in the field of foreign affairs. Nowhere has that been more apparent than in discussions of nuclear weapons and their possible use. But surely actions which literally threaten the survival of our civilization have a moral dimension. More and more attention, therefore, should be, and I believe will be, directed to the moral implications of our nuclear strategy.

The Catholic bishops of the United States have begun to do so. In a seminal paper published in 1983, they "provisionally" accepted the morality of the West's present strategy of nuclear deterrence.[6] I agree with their conclusion. In the face of the Soviet force of approximately 25,000 nuclear weapons, I see no alternative to NATO's maintaining an invulnerable retaliation force— a force so clearly capable of responding to a nuclear strike on the West with a devastating blow on the Soviet Union as to deter them from initiating such a strike. We have no choice. Therefore, questions of the morality of a deterrent policy, in present circumstances, do not arise.

However, the superpowers have translated their deterrent strategy into war plans involving the exchange of thousands of nuclear warheads. One does not have to accept the concept of nuclear winter to recognize that such an exchange, through atmospheric effects, would place in jeopardy the very survival of many of the other nations of the world. And this is a moral issue. We should expect, therefore, that in future years the Brazils, the Indias and the Swedens will demand that we change our strategy, our war plans and our deployment of nuclear forces.

Finally, there is one other moral dimension of the Cold War we should examine. As I have said, at present, pursuing a policy of deterrence, even though it places the survival of our nation at risk, raises no moral issue, because we have no choice. But in the future, if we perceive a chance to end the Cold War—to remove the risk to our survival—are we not bound to pursue it? Surely the answer is Yes. I proceed next to examine whether the United States and the Soviet Union are facing that opportunity.

IV

Gorbachev's Changes in Soviet Domestic and Foreign Policy:

THEIR CAUSES AND THEIR RELATIONSHIP TO THE COLD WAR

$\mathbf{M}$ikhail Gorbachev represents a profound break with the Soviet past. He is attempting to introduce deep and broad transformations into Soviet domestic and foreign policy. Although the inefficiency of the Soviet economy and the ineffectiveness of and risks associated with Soviet foreign policy are problems that have faced successive Soviet leaders for decades, Gorbachev is the first to seek to address these problems at their roots. At the heart of his approach is his belief that Soviet interests in the twenty-first century can best be served in a peaceful international environment, an environment that features reduced superpower tension and increased U.S.–Soviet cooperation.

In short, Gorbachev is presenting the West with an unprecedented opportunity to redefine the basic assumptions and conditions of East–West relations. In his words and in his deeds, he appears to be offering the West the chance to end the Cold War.

The "New Thinking" in Soviet Policy

Among the myriad of changes introduced in the Soviet Union at Gorbachev's initiative are at least four that bear directly on East–West relations and offer new opportunities to reduce tension.

First and foremost, Gorbachev has launched a fundamental reassessment of the Soviet view of national-security and Soviet geopolitical objectives. Second, related to the current restructuring of the Soviet economy, is Moscow's new desire to break down the insularity of the Soviet economic structure and integrate it—technologically and financially—into the increasingly interdependent global economy. Third, the General Secretary has introduced preliminary, though still significant, liberalization of Soviet human-rights laws. Lastly, and related to all three of the above changes, is the remarkable Soviet rejection of a number of fundamental tenets of Marxist-Leninist ideology in both domestic and foreign policy. Each of these major developments will be addressed below.

Gorbachev's Reassessment of the Requirements of Security

Before Mikhail Gorbachev's appointment in March 1985 as General Secretary of the Communist Party of the Soviet Union, Moscow's view of national security appeared to assume that the USSR could guarantee its security only to the extent that other nations felt insecure. Soviet foreign and defense policy, seemingly designed to heighten the insecurity of states on the Soviet periphery, the countries of Western Europe and the United States, was likened to a zero-sum game in which Moscow gained the security lost by others. Since 1985, however, Gorbachev has sought to redefine Soviet perceptions of national security by introducing his so-called New Thinking in Soviet foreign-policy calculations.

The New Thinking on foreign policy features at least three concepts strongly at odds with the traditional Soviet approach: (1) A nation's security interests should be pursued through diplomacy, not military threats or the use of force. (2) One nation's security cannot be guaranteed at the expense of the security of others; security cannot be pursued unilaterally—it must be strengthened in cooperation with other states. (3) International organizations and bilateral efforts can serve to solve regional and global problems.

Gorbachev has consistently repeated each of these themes in a number of speeches, articles and press conferences since 1985. I will, in this section, discuss

109

them in turn, and then point out important specifics of
the New Thinking that Gorbachev has applied to two
areas of particular interest to the United States—Eastern Europe and the Third World.

Security Through Diplomacy, Not Military Means.
The point that Gorbachev returns to more than any
other when discussing foreign policy is his belief that
modern military technologies, specifically nuclear
weapons, have rendered war an inadmissible means of
advancing a nation's security interests. There is a lack
of proportionality in nuclear war, according to Gorbachev: the destruction would far outweigh any con-
ceivable political goal. And any war between the United
States and the Soviet Union contains within it the seeds
of a possible unlimited nuclear war.

August 1985: "You asked me what is the primary
thing that defines Soviet–American relations. I
think it is the immutable fact that whether we like
one another or not, we can either survive or perish
only together."[1]

February 1986: "The nature of current weaponry
leaves no state with any hope of defending itself
using solely military-technical means ... Ensuring security is becoming more and more a political task, and it can be accomplished only by
political means."[2]

February 1986: "Objective ... conditions have
taken shape in which confrontation between cap-

italism and socialism can proceed *only and exclusively in forms of peaceful competition and peaceful contest.*"[3]

Fall 1986: "The fundamental principle of the new political outlook is very simple: *nuclear war cannot be a means of achieving political, economic, ideological or any other goals.* This conclusion is truly revolutionary, for it means discarding the traditional notions of war and peace."[4]

Fall 1986: "It is crystal clear that in the world we live in, the world of nuclear weapons, any attempt to use them to solve Soviet–American problems would spell suicide."[5]

December 1988: "The use or threat of force no longer ... can be an instrument of foreign policy."[6]

Soviet military authors have also adopted Gorbachev's formulation of this point. Four months after the February 1986 Party Congress, a confidential journal of the Soviet General Staff ran a lead editorial echoing Gorbachev's assessment:

Security in the nuclear age must be evaluated differently. Assessing security is more and more becoming a political task. It can only be resolved by political means through detente, disarmament, strengthening confidence, and developing international cooperation. It is unthinkable and even criminal to seek to resolve the problems of security in an arms race, perfecting the "shield" and the "sword."[7]

Security Cannot Be Pursued Unilaterally, Only Co-operatively. Directly related to Gorbachev's assessment of the utility of military force is his conception of the cooperative, or "mutual," nature of security. Gorbachev has asserted repeatedly that the Soviet Union has rejected its earlier espousal of unilateral security:

> February 1986: "In the context of the relations between the USSR and the USA, security can only be mutual, and if we take international relations as a whole it can only be universal . . . It is vital that all should feel equally secure, for the fears and anxieties of the nuclear age generate unpredictability in politics."[8]

> July 1986: In a speech in Vladivostok, Gorbachev argued that the Soviets "require a radical break with traditions of political thinking." He rejected an "egotistical attempt to strengthen security at someone else's expense."[9]

> August 1986: "Today one's own security cannot be ensured without taking into account the security of other states and peoples. There can be no genuine security unless it is equal for all and comprehensive. To think otherwise is to live in a world of illusions, in a world of self-deception."[10]

Cooperative Efforts to Solve Global and Regional Problems. In addition to seeking to reduce U.S.–Soviet tensions, Gorbachev has proposed strengthening mechanisms for defusing potential third-area conflicts. He has placed particular emphasis on the United Nations, multilateral conferences on regional problems, and increased U.S.–Soviet cooperation:

February 1987: "Settlement of regional conflicts is a must of our time . . . We say, Let us search and act together. This applies to the Iran–Iraq war, the Central American crisis, the Afghan problem and the situation in the South of Africa and in Indochina. The main thing is to honor the rights of the people to decide their own destiny themselves, not to interfere in the internal affairs of the other states."[11]

In a September 1987 *Pravda* article, Gorbachev outlined an eleven-point proposal for expanding the authority of the United Nations on such issues as military conflicts, international economic relations, terrorism, and global environmental issues. He suggested granting the UN Security Council greatly broadened powers in the spheres of conflict resolution and the verification of arms-control and peace treaties.[12]

A week later, Soviet Foreign Minister Eduard Shevardnadze, in a speech to the UN General Assembly, called for a United Nations naval presence in the Persian Gulf to ensure freedom of navigation there.[13]

In October 1987, the Soviets announced their

intention to pay in full their outstanding $225 million debt to the United Nations.[14]

Gorbachev, in his December 1988 speech to the United Nations, suggested that the UN should create a wide variety of multilateral councils designed to address such problems as the global environment and the Third World debt crisis. He also proposed an "international peace corps" to deal with human and social problems in war-torn Afghanistan.

Both the United States and the Soviet Union have stressed in summit meetings the importance of cooperating on regional issues. This idea was pursued during three days of talks at the beginning of September 1988 between Michael H. Armacost, U.S. Undersecretary of State for Political Affairs, and Yuli M. Vorontsov, First Deputy Foreign Minister of the USSR. Both sides have stated that regional problem-solving is the second most active area of U.S.–Soviet discussions (after arms control), and Armacost cited such "notable successes" as the Soviet withdrawal from Afghanistan, the Iran–Iraq cease-fire, the tentative schedule for Namibian independence and the future withdrawal of Vietnamese troops from Cambodia.[15] Although such Soviet initiatives reflect, at least in part, Moscow's desire to reduce the burden of its economic and military commitments abroad, Soviet foreign policy is without question moving in directions that the United States has sought to encourage for quite some time.

Application of the New Thinking to Eastern Europe and the Third World

We can already see the effect of the New Thinking on Soviet relations with Eastern Europe. Moscow appears to be moving away from its earlier demands for authoritarian control over the region. Gorbachev has stressed the "independence" of East European states. He has refrained from supporting "proletarian internationalism," the foundation of the Brezhnev Doctrine that reserved the right for the Soviet Union to invade socialist countries that stray from the Soviet line:

First of all the entire framework of political relations between the socialist countries must be absolute independence. This is the view held by the leaders of all fraternal countries. The independence of each Party, its sovereign right to decide the issues facing its country and its responsibility to its nation are the unquestionable principles.[16]

We do not think that we know the best answers to all questions. We are far from asking anyone to copy us. Every socialist country is unique, and fraternal parties shape their policies proceeding from national specifics.[17]

No party has a monopoly on truth. Some problems that are now priorities in the Soviet Union have already been solved in other socialist countries, or they are solving them in their own way.[18]

East European leaders report that meetings with Gorbachev are characterized by "genuine give-and-take," which differs significantly from their talks with earlier Soviet leaders.[19] This lends credibility to the statements quoted above.

Judging by his proposals for conventional arms control, Gorbachev does not appear to believe that the West will attack Eastern Europe. Perceiving that the national-security threats to Eastern Europe have diminished, Gorbachev seems to believe that he can afford to offer Eastern Europe increased autonomy and improved ties with the West. Based on the experience of the last two or three decades, the easing of tension between the superpowers is a prerequisite for increased East European autonomy.

The application of the new foreign policy is also visible in Soviet behavior toward the Third World. Here too the Soviets are showing unmistakable signs of reassessing their goals, the potential gains to be made and the extent of their involvement. As a result of this reassessment of costs and benefits, the Soviets have reduced their involvement in several Third World conflicts, including those in southern Africa and Southeast Asia. Moreover, many analysts have pointed out that Moscow appears to be initiating no new economic or military support of Third World socialist regimes. Robert Legvold has written that, in contrast to his predecessors, Gorbachev finds the Third World "a hopeless and tragic arena, not a region of hope and promise."[20]

A recent article in the Soviet foreign-policy journal

ROBERT S. McNAMARA

International Affairs clearly spells out the reasoning
behind the Soviet reassessment of activities in the Third
World and lays out the implications of that reassessment: Soviet commitments have been too costly, results
have been meager, and therefore Third World regimes
can expect far less support from the USSR in the future.
The article states:

> [Western spokesmen can] now persuade leaders of the
> Third World countries more successfuly than in the past
> that the socialist economic system as it exists in the
> Soviet Union is inferior to the capitalist system.

> Soviet assistance to the developing countries, both eco-
> nomic and military, too often brings only fleeting re-
> sults, mainly in the period of the struggle for power and
> in the first years of the existence of a progressive gov-
> ernment. Subsequently, in the period of regular eco-
> nomic development, young states are beginning to turn
> increasingly to the West.

> A heavier burden of expenditures on foreign policy and
> defense . . . will, undoubtedly, damage the [Soviet] ci-
> vilian economy and jeopardize the program of its mod-
> ernization. . . . Besides, it may lower living standards,
> and the reserves of patience in this field are not inex-
> haustible.

> We should display more selectivity in identifying our
> goals and commitments abroad. In particular, it would
> be expedient to gradually abandon our global rivalry
> with the USA and refrain from the costly support of
> unpopular regimes, political movements, parties, etc.

117

The Soviet Union has come to the point when it is necessary to adopt a doctrine which would give the country a respite needed to restructure its economy and make the socialist path of development more attractive. . . . The price of our past mistakes is very high. We no longer have the right to repeat them.[21]

The Results of the New Thinking in Soviet Foreign and Defense Policy

Before turning to the New Thinking as it applies to the economy, to human rights and to Marxist-Leninist ideology, I should stress that in foreign and defense policy it has manifested itself not only in words but in deeds as well. An early and important example of Soviet flexibility and willingness to consider new solutions to old problems was, of course, the Soviet signing of the Intermediate-range Nuclear Forces (INF) Treaty in December of 1987. The terms of the Reagan "double-zero" option were rejected for years by successive Soviet leaders; only under Gorbachev did the option seem even remotely negotiable.

By signing the INF Treaty, the Soviets acquiesced in two very important precedents that will have major implications in the conventional-arms negotiations and in the Strategic Arms Reduction Talks (START) as well. First, Moscow agreed to deeply asymmetrical cuts in nuclear weapons in Europe; that is, it consented to remove far more weapons than the United States. Second, the principle of intrusive on-site inspections was established by the treaty. Although Moscow for decades resisted such inspections as part of any arms-control regime, they will now be regarded as the rule, not the exception.

With respect to conventional arms, equally dramatic moves have been made. Soviet leaders have clearly expressed their willingness to agree to arms accords that require deeper cuts by the Soviet Union than by the United States. The March 1989 Soviet proposal that opened the Conventional Forces in Europe (CFE) talks in Vienna was surprisingly close to the opening NATO proposal. The Soviets called for initial cuts of both sides' forces to equal levels approximately 10 to 15 percent below what either side possesses now. To achieve these levels, the Warsaw Pact countries would have to reduce many weapon systems much more drastically than would NATO. At the opening session of the talks, NATO proposed cuts on the order of 5 to 10 percent. Both sides were reported to be encouraged by the similarity of the initial proposals.[22]

The CFE negotiations take place in the wake of Gorbachev's dramatic December 1988 speech at the United Nations in which he announced that the Soviet Union would reduce its armed forces, over the next two years, by 500,000 troops, 10,000 tanks, 8,500 artillery tubes and 800 combat aircraft. As part of these reductions, Moscow will withdraw a total of six tank divisions from Eastern Europe, including four from East Germany. These will be among the most highly trained troops in the Soviet Army. In addition, Gorbachev has pledged to remove and disband the only air assault brigade now stationed in East Germany and the only assault battalion now in Hungary. These reductions in offensive forces in Eastern Europe are strong evidence that Gorbachev does indeed intend to restructure Warsaw Pact deployments and strategy in order to support purely defensive aims.[23]

Following his announcement of troop reductions, Gorbachev declared in January 1989 that the Soviet Union plans to reduce its defense spending by 14.2 percent and cut the production of Soviet arms by 19.5 percent. While it is notoriously difficult to monitor and measure Soviet defense spending, and while the cuts announced by Gorbachev are extremely large, the consistency of his entire approach lends credence to this declaration.

Similar reductions in hardware and spending announced by other members of the Warsaw Pact, when fully carried out, will also reduce the intensity of the offensive threat faced by NATO:

> East Germany has announced a reduction of 10,000 active-duty troops from its total of 170,000; the destruction or conversion to civilian use of 600 of its 3,000 tanks; the deactivation of 50 of 350 combat aircraft; and the reduction of military spending by 10 percent.
>
> Czechoslovakia will cut 12,000 active-duty troops from its current total of 145,000; deactivate 850 tanks, 165 armored vehicles, and 51 combat aircraft; and reduce defense spending by 15 percent.

Hungary has pledged to demobilize 9,300 active-duty troops, withdraw 251 tanks and cut military spending by 17 percent.

Bulgaria will cut 10,000 active-duty troops; withdraw 200 tanks, 200 artillery tubes and 20 combat aircraft; and reduce defense spending by 12 percent.[24]

One cannot persuasively argue that these cuts are unimportant or designed merely to deceive the West. The East European reductions follow closely the Soviet pattern of reducing the most offensive elements in the Warsaw Pact arsenal. While it remains to be seen just how these cuts are implemented, they will almost certainly have an important dampening effect on the offensive threat facing NATO.

Another signal development in Soviet foreign and defense policy has been the withdrawal of Soviet forces from Afghanistan. After pledging to remove the troops, the Soviets did just that in remarkably short order, thus healing what Gorbachev called a "bleeding wound." A Soviet withdrawal from Afghanistan, in the wake of failure to pacify the *mujaheddin,* was unthinkable only one or two years ago. It is the first postwar example of Soviet acquiescence in the defeat of a Communist regime on the Soviet border. As such, it constitutes further evidence of Gorbachev's commitment to reducing or eliminating costly and draining foreign operations and to improving Soviet relations with both the West and China.

A number of additional developments undermine the arguments of those who say Gorbachev's deeds do not match his words, that he has altered neither the goals nor the instruments of Soviet foreign policy. Soviet relations with China are changing dramatically. At the time of this writing, top Soviet and Chinese officials are scheduled to meet for the first time in three decades. Progress that seemed impossible a short time ago has been made on a variety of Sino–Soviet issues. Moscow announced in March 1989 that it will withdraw 75 percent of its troops in Mongolia (on the border with China), including all airborne detachments. Mongolia itself, a staunch ally of Moscow, is reducing its troop level by 13,000 and its military budget by 11 percent.

Even more dramatic actions are supporting the announced changes in Moscow's relations with Eastern Europe. These actions go to the very heart of the origin of the Cold War. The Cold War originated, in part, as a result of Soviet dominance in the region and the Soviet refusal to allow multiparty systems and free elections. Now, for the first time since the end of World War II, the Soviets appear to be allowing the peaceful development of legitimate opposition to the ruling Communist powers. In February of 1989, Hungary approved plans for its first multiparty election in forty years— obviously with Moscow's approval, tacit or otherwise. Similarly, in March 1989, Poland announced plans to reestablish its Senate, abolished in 1956. Although many unresolved details remain, the entire Polish Senate will be chosen in free elections, and its powers may be significant.

In addition, Gorbachev has presided over withdrawals and retreats by Soviet "proxy" forces. An agreement has been reached that provides for the withdrawal of Cuban forces from Angola within three years, and in the view of most observers it is nearly certain that Vietnamese forces will soon begin a withdrawal from Cambodia.

Gorbachev is clearly "demilitarizing" and "democratizing" Soviet foreign policy. We can no longer hold to the view that his policies have changed only in style and not in substance.

Moscow's Desire to Increase Its Involvement in the World Economy

In addition to the New Thinking in Soviet foreign and defense policy, the Soviets are making major changes as well in their international economic policies. They clearly recognize that the twenty-first century will be a period of dramatic technological change which will spread rapidly among nations participating in the global economy—which today they are not.

Gorbachev has sought to improve Soviet trade opportunities and integrate the Soviet economic structure into the world economy in four ways: by streamlining the Soviet foreign-trade apparatus; by obtaining access to Western financial institutions; by strongly encouraging joint ventures with Western businesses; and by petitioning for, or considering, Soviet membership in international economic organizations, including the General Agreement on Trade and Tariffs (GATT), the World Bank and the International Monetary Fund.

At the Washington summit in December 1987 Gorbachev made the following statements:

> As to economic relations with America, I simply do not know how we can tolerate any further such a state of our economic and trade ties.

> We could become useful to each other. We are convinced that American business can launch its operations in the Soviet Union with benefit to itself.

> If anyone is prepared to particiapte with us and to help us while benefiting himself, we invite him to do so. We will be looking for approaches and creating the conditions necessary for such cooperation.

> Everyone willing to join in will have the support of both the government and the political leadership.[25]

Soviet Progress on Human-Rights Issues

In addition to its application to political and economic cooperation, Gorbachev's New Thinking has also begun to be applied in the area of human rights. Major cases, such as the well-known human-rights activist Andrey Sakharov's release from exile and his subsequent Western travel, have received extensive coverage, but movement has taken place on other fronts, too.

Over six hundred political prisoners have been released in the last two years, and the Soviets have made public a commitment to eliminate the brutal practice of subjecting dissidents to psychological "treatment."

Restrictions on the study and practice of religion are being eased. Over 100,000 Bibles were recently imported for sale to Soviet citizens, and in the fall of 1988 Moscow ended the Soviet ban on the teaching of Hebrew.[26]

The Soviet legal code is being revised to eliminate restrictions on a wide variety of political and other activity. Catch-all laws prohibiting "anti-Soviet behavior" that have been used in the past to prosecute dissidents will be eliminated. The jurisdiction of the International Court of Justice at The Hague as regards the interpretation and implementation of agreements on human rights will be accepted as binding.

In 1987, emigration of Soviet Jews was up almost nine times over the 1986 total (8,149 in 1987, up from 914 in 1986), and the 1988 total (19,200) more than doubled the 1987 figure. An Israeli official has estimated that the number of Jews leaving the Soviet Union in 1989 will reach forty thousand.[27]

In Gorbachev's December 1988 speech to the United Nations, he pledged that in 1989 laws will be written into the Soviet code guaranteeing freedom of expression and complete freedom from religious persecution. He added that the law prohibiting emigration of a person with knowledge of state secrets will be modified to include "strictly warranted time limitations."

It is correct to say that Soviet citizens continue to live under the weight of a great many onerous restrictions and prohibitions, but the initial steps to reduce those restrictions have been significant and contrast sharply with the former Soviet disregard for the issue of human rights.

Acknowledging Moscow's progress, the Reagan Administration, in one of its final official acts, approved U.S. participation in a human-rights conference to be held in Moscow in 1991.

The Breakdown of Classical Marxist-Leninist Ideology

Gorbachev's New Thinking in foreign and domestic policy has been accompanied by a rejection of some of the most basic concepts of the traditional Marxist-Leninist assessment of economics and international relations. It is not clear which came first. We do not know whether the revision of ideology preceded the rethinking of Soviet foreign and domestic priorities, or whether the realization of the need for major policy changes necessitated revisions of ideology. At this point, however, both processes are evolving in parallel, and each sustains the momentum of the other.

Regarding international relations, the revision of ideology has struck at the basic foundations of Marxism-Leninism. First, contrary to Marx's most fundamental precept, capitalism is not expected to decline any time in the near future, nor should socialists necessarily seek to accelerate that decline. Soviet commentators unanimously agreed in the 1970s that détente was the result of U.S. realization of its ultimate decline; they believed that Nixon's "retrenchment" reflected an understanding that the United States would have to accommodate itself to its inability to change and to its eclipse by the Soviet Union. The current Soviet line is remarkably different. The new party program declares that "present-day capitalism differs in many respects from what it was . . . even in the middle of the twentieth century." And Gorbachev stated at the Twenty-seventh Party Congress:

> The present stage . . . does not lead to any absolute stagnation of capitalism and does not rule out possible growth of its economy and the mastery of new scientific and technical trends. . . . [The capitalists' situation] allows for sustaining concrete economic, military, political and other positions and in some cases even for possible . . . regaining of what had been lost before. . . . The existing complex of economic, politico-military and other common interests of the three centers of power [the United States, Western Europe and Japan] can hardly be expected to break up.[28]

Second, the supremacy and inevitability of socialism have been subject to question under Gorbachev. "We are far from regarding our approach as the only correct

127

one. We have," he wrote in *Perestroika* in 1987, "no universal solutions."[29] Moreover, human failure, according to Gorbachev, could lead to the downfall of the Soviet Union and of socialism as a whole: "the historic fate of the country and the positions of socialism in the modern world depend to a large extent on how we manage things from now on."[30] In addition, Soviet theorists have acknowledged that pro-socialist revolutionary changes in the Third World have been slowed, halted, and even reversed.[31]

Gorbachev's New Thinking has also broken with classical Marxism-Leninism by declaring that conflict need not be considered the norm in the international system. Gorbachev has done away with Marx and Lenin's assertion that the interests of capitalist and socialist states must be contradictory.

April 1985: "Confrontation is not an inborn defect in our relations. It is rather an anomaly. Its continuation is not inevitable at all."[32]

April 1985: "We do not think that underlying the present-day tensions in these relations is some fatal clash of the national interests of both countries. On the contrary, our peoples can gain much from the development of broad and fruitful cooperation. . . . The difference in the social systems, in the ideology of our countries, is not cause for curtailing relations, much less for kindling hatred."[33]

In *Perestroika*, Gorbachev wrote that the concept of class struggle—perhaps the basic Marxist conception—should be replaced by "peaceful co-existence" and mutual interdependence.[34]

Gorbachev has also stressed that the "main contradiction" of the contemporary period is not the Marxist contradiction between socialism and capitalism but the contradiction between war and peace.[35]

The General Secretary has emphasized "the new style of [the Soviets'] international activities," their "genuine renunciation of ideologizing state-to-state relations."[36] By undermining classic Marxist-Leninist doctrine and by suggesting a pragmatic twentieth-century alternative, he has opened the way for a far-reaching discussion of mutual security and cooperation.

Ideological revision is also taking place on the issue of the domestic Soviet economy. The most important innovations in this sphere are Gorbachev's efforts to introduce more market-oriented incentives into the Soviet economy. Replacing "command" methods with market mechanisms has long been regarded as ideologically untenable, but Gorbachev has made such efforts the core of his attempts to restructure the economy. Vadim Medvedev, chief of ideology in the Kremlin hierarchy, has been in the forefront of the efforts to legitimize market mechanisms in Soviet economic thinking. The *Pravda* report of a speech Medvedev delivered on March 1, 1989, said:

> The market, he noted, can be built into the most diverse socioeconomic systems and can serve them effi-

ciently. . . . Attempts to do without it for the sake of
"purity of the socialist idea" inevitably result in a swell-
ing of the bureaucratic apparatus, dominance of the
supplier over the consumer, and flourishing monopo-
lism.[37]

This is very strong criticism of what in fact has been
Soviet policy and doctrine for the last half century or
more.

Origins of the New Thinking

Before concluding my discussion of the New Thinking, I want to consider its origins; they will help answer
the question "Is this but a passing phase?"

Gorbachev's understanding of three interrelated phe-
nomena has, I believe, prompted his new approach to
Soviet foreign and domestic policy. The three phenom-
ena have been unfolding for years, even decades, but
no previous Soviet leader has shown the understanding
or the energy necessary to accommodate Soviet policy
to the rapidly changing environment.

First, of course, is the worsening of the state of the
Soviet economy. Declining Soviet growth rates, and the
realization that the East–West technological gap was
growing, prompted Gorbachev to launch reforms that
are designed in part to allow the Soviet economy to catch
up in the increasingly technologically oriented environment. Many Soviet officials currently acknowledge that
they are seeking to create a calm international environ-

ment—and peaceful relations with the United States—
so that attention and resources can be diverted toward
necessary improvements in the domestic economy.

Second, as I emphasized in the previous chapter, the
Soviets have shown an increasing understanding of the
risk of nuclear war. Soviet officials—including Gorbachev—have begun to state that the greatest danger
to Soviet security comes not from the United States,
but from the massive arsenals of nuclear weapons themselves.

The third phenomenon, to which I will also refer at
the end of this chapter, is a growing understanding of
the interdependent nature of the modern world—politically, technologically, economically, environmentally—and a realization of the pitfalls of attempting to
"go it alone" into the twenty-first century.

In each of these areas, which I will discuss more fully
below, the benefits envisioned by the New Thinking
are dependent on better relations with the West and a
more peaceful environment in which to undertake Soviet policy initiatives.

The Soviet Economy

Even a brief discussion of the problems of the Soviet
economy will demonstrate why the Soviets are seeking
reduced tension with the United States and increased
East–West cooperation. At the time Gorbachev as-
sumed power in the USSR, the Soviet economy was
mired in a decade-long slump; for the period 1976–85,

131

the average GNP growth rate was just over 2 percent per year, including less than 1.5 percent in 1984 and zero growth in the first quarter of 1985.[38] Gorbachev surprised Western analysts in a speech to a Communist Party plenum in February 1988 when he said that, omitting the "nonproductive" domestic sales of alcohol and foreign sales of oil, "over four five-year-plan periods we knew no increase in the absolute increment of the national income, and it even began declining in the early eighties."[39]

Not only had growth come to a halt; the quality of Soviet industrial goods was acknowledged to be extremely shoddy as well. Gorbachev's chief economic adviser, Abel Agenbegyan, noted that "in machine-tool construction and instrument-making, 86 percent and 83 percent of output, respectively, are below world standards."[40] Gorbachev has commented endlessly on the sorry state of the Soviet economy. He emphasizes the fact that, although the economy itself is enormous, Soviet work methods are inexcusably inefficient:

> An absurd situation was developing. The Soviet Union, the world's biggest producer of steel, raw materials, fuel and energy, has shortfalls in them due to waste or inefficient use. One of the biggest producers of grain for food, it nevertheless has to buy millions of tons of grain a year for fodder. We have the largest number of doctors and hospital beds per thousand of the population and, at the same time, there are glaring shortcomings in our health services.[41]

Gorbachev's Early Efforts. Gorbachev's first year in office was devoted almost exclusively to improving what he called the "human factors" responsible for the economic decline. He hoped to eradicate absenteeism, corruption, incompetence, and drunkenness on the job. The laws and decrees of May 1985, for example, drastically limited the production and sale of alcohol and instituted stiff penalties for public drunkenness. During this period, Gorbachev was not yet emphasizing *perestroika* (restructuring), but was stressing only *uskoreniye* (acceleration). The latter term indicates that Gorbachev did not yet perceive the need for a radical reorganization of the economy; he believed that the essential elements were in place but were being inefficiently exploited.

Gorbachev himself has recently acknowledged his misunderstanding of the severity of the problem. Referring to his first year in office, he stated in June 1988 that the Soviet leadership "underestimated the extent and gravity of the deformations and the stagnation of the preceding period. There was a lot we simply did not know and did not see until now: the neglect in various fields of the economy turned out to be more serious then we have initially thought."[42]

In 1986 and the first half of 1987, Gorbachev introduced a number of uncoordinated and scattered ad-hoc measures. The most important of these reforms were directed at (1) streamlining certain planning and finance procedures in some industrial sectors, (2) introducing self-financing of enterprises, and (3) instituting minor changes in the national economic-planning mechanism. The aim of the reforms was to increase and encourage autonomy on the part of certain important industrial enterprises. Gorbachev was seeking to ease the heavy burden of central planning on important producers of industrial and consumer goods.

The piecemeal reforms, however, could not be expected to take hold in an economy that continued to be largely centrally planned and stagnant. Agenbegyan compared the sluggish economy and the scattered reforms to "a living organism when you try to make a transplant. The rest of the organism resists and fights against it. We realize we have to make a much more comprehensive approach."[43] As late as March 1987, the U.S. Central Intelligence Agency and Defense Intelligence Agency wrote that "despite [Gorbachev's] frenetic efforts over the past two years, we still do not see a viable, integrated plan for modernization."[44]

The June 1987 Central Committee Plenum. A comprehensive, coordinated plan for radically restructuring the Soviet economy was unveiled by Gorbachev at the June 1987 Central Committee plenum. The most important goal of the plan is to limit the role of central planning in all sectors of the economy to long-range, national planning, and to authorize enterprises to conduct day-to-day operations as they see fit.

The directives of the June plenum seek to:

1. Replace administrative management mechanisms with economic instruments. Centrally determined annual plans are eliminated, and enterprises will be forced to earn a profit or go bankrupt.

2. Transfer sweeping authority from the central ministries to the enterprises themselves. Enterprises are authorized to hire and fire workers, determine suppliers and customers, and adjust output mix according to their needs.

3. Implement new systems of quality control, price formation, and competition. Private and cooperative economic activities are encouraged in some sectors.

4. Increase the role of money, credit and profit in the economic systems. Money is to become a true medium of exchange.[45]

These changes in the Soviet economic structure are unprecedented and truly revolutionary. The reforms substantially increase the interest of workers in the management of their enterprises and wholly reshape the power of enterprise managers. Although the supporters of reform face an enormously difficult path in the years ahead, Gorbachev hopes to make the Soviet economy competitive in the high-tech twenty-first century.

The foreign-policy implications of Soviet economic reform are clear. Gorbachev acknowledges that he is attempting to create a calm international environment in order to be able to devote maximum attention to the Soviet Union's domestic economic woes. Soviet theorists have acknowledged that Gorbachev's drive for U.S.–Soviet cooperation and "mutual security" is a direct result of the dire economic situation in which the USSR finds itself:

Yevgeniy Primakov, director of the prestigious Institute of the World Economy and International Relations, in July 1987: "But why did this indisputable, correct idea begin to materialize intensively in our country only after the April [1985] plenary session of the CPSU Central Committee? . . . Perhaps the organic link between our country's domestic policy and its foreign policy has never before been as manifest as it is today. . . . Given the emphasis on the sharp speedup in the economic and social development of the Soviet Union, the need for optimizing the ratio between productive expenditures and military expenditures necessary for the country's reliable security has been manifest as never before."[46]

Gorbachev in August 1985: "It was said justly that foreign policy is an extension of domestic policy. Since this is so, I would ask you to give some thought to the following: Since we are undertaking such challenging domestic plans, what external conditions can we be interested in? I leave it to you to provide the answer."[47]

Gorbachev in February 1987: "Our international

policy is more than ever determined by our domestic policy, by our interest in concentrating on
constructive endeavors to improve our country.
This is why we need lasting peace, predictability
and constructiveness in international relations."[48]

In the past, Soviet leaders encouraged and took advantage of the image of a hostile and belligerent United
States in order to exhort Soviet citizens to work harder
and to justify high levels of spending on military hardware; a hostile enemy could be blamed for shortcomings
in the Soviet economy. Now, however, Gorbachev appears to want to reverse this equation. Instead of in-
flating the image of the enemy in order to justify the
poor domestic economic situation, he is moving to de-
flate the image, reduce tensions and defuse conflicts in
order to allow a reduction of military spending and increased investment in the civilian economy. The former
need for an enemy as an excuse for shortcomings at
home may now have disappeared. Reducing the perceived threat from abroad allows more resources to be
diverted inward.

Increased Soviet Attention to the Risk of Nuclear War

In Chapter III, I described the meeting held in Moscow in January of this year to review the Cuban Missile
Crisis, in order to emphasize my belief that under Gorbachev the Soviets have begun to demonstrate a greater

understanding of the monumental risks implicit in the massive nuclear arsenals of the superpowers. The Soviets, in private conversations and in public treatments of the issue, have made clear their belief that superpower confrontations do not lend themselves to a high degree of control. Their experience in crises—particularly the Cuban Missile Crisis—has led them to believe that crises are inherently unstable situations that cannot be confidently controlled or managed by either side. They have begun to argue, therefore, that rather than relying on crisis management, the superpowers must devote their greatest attention to crisis prevention. Crisis prevention must be the superpowers' highest security priority.

Indeed, Gorbachev and other Soviets have put forth the proposition that the greatest security threat to the Soviet Union—and to the world as a whole—comes not from the United States, but from the existence of nuclear weapons themselves. Although previous Soviet leaders have asserted that strategic parity can guarantee the nonuse of nuclear weapons, Gorbachev believes that as levels of nuclear weapons rise, the likelihood of their use increases:

February 1986: "Continuation of the nuclear arms race will inevitably heighten this . . . threat and may bring it to a point where even parity will cease to be a factor of military-political deterrence."[49]

August 1986: "The 'balance of terror' is ceasing

138

to be a deterrent factor. And not only because terror itself is a poor counselor that can prompt actions with unforeseeable consequences. That terror is a direct participant in the arms race: intensifying mistrust and suspicion, it forms a vicious circle of growing tension."[50]

February 1987: Deterrence "may at any time become a death sentence to mankind. The bigger the nuclear arsenals, the less chance they will obey our will."[51]

A major goal of Gorbachev's foreign policy, as a result, is to enlist the cooperation of the United States in the creation of a more stable world.

Fall 1987: "We know and take into account the great role played by the United States in the modern world, value the Americans' contribution to world civilization, . . . and realize that without that country it is impossible to remove the threat of nuclear catastrophe and secure a lasting peace."[52]

November 1987: "Since an alliance between a socialist country and capitalist states proved possible in the past, when the threat of Fascism arose, does this not suggest a lesson for the present, for today's world which faces the threat of nuclear catastrophe and the need to ensure safe nuclear power production and overcome the danger to the environment?"[53]

In December 1987, Gorbachev referred to the "special responsibility of the Soviet Union and the United States for finding realistic ways to prevent military confrontation and building a safer world."[54]

Gorbachev appears to believe not only that U.S.–Soviet cooperation is necessary, but that it is possible as well. In the past year, he has suggested several times that the United States can be regarded as a productive partner:

In an October 1987 speech, Gorbachev noted that American rhetoric is extremely belligerent, but that "a few days after" the tough-sounding speeches U.S. actions are more businesslike.[55]

At the Washington summit in December 1987, Gorbachev was asked whether he had been able to change any of President Reagan's ideas about the Soviet Union. He answered, "Well, I guess Mr. Reagan's views have changed for the better, as have mine."[56]

At the May 30, 1988, summit dinner in Moscow, Gorbachev praised President Reagan for his "realism," a code word long used by the Soviets to indicate American willingness to deal with the Soviet Union. "I like the notion of realism," Gorbachev announced, "and I also like the fact that you, Mr. President, have lately been uttering it more and more often."[57]

By February of 1989, Gorbachev was arguing that major accomplishments had been achieved by the New Thinking in Soviet foreign policy. He stated that the new Soviet emphasis on dialogue and political solutions to multilateral problems had resulted in positive gains for the Soviets and the world. He described the Soviet course as making "maximum use of political means for defusing international tensions, attaining mutual understanding with the West and resolving the most complicated international differences through dialogue, negotiations and the search for reasonable compromises."

This course, closely related to our profound, far-reaching domestic changes, has made it possible to start removing such a large rock hanging over humankind as the Soviet–American confrontation. Improved relations between the USSR and the United States have achieved a breakthrough in the entire world process.[58]

Soviet Recognition of the Interdependence of Modern Nations

Gorbachev's perception of the mutual nature of security and the need for increased U.S.–Soviet cooperation to reduce the likelihood of nuclear war is founded on the new Soviet view of the interdependent character of the contemporary world. The Soviets have begun to discuss the increasingly complex nature of the world's economic, environmental, political and military interrelationships and have called for greater cooperation in

141

all these areas. The world is small and fragile, according to Gorbachev, and its parts are linked together for better or for worse:

> April 1987: "Today, world nations are interdependent, like mountain climbers attached to one rope. They can either climb together to the summit or all fall into the abyss."[59]
>
> Fall 1987: "The Soviet Union alone cannot resolve all these issues. And we are not ashamed to repeat this, calling for international cooperation. We say with full responsibility, casting away the false considerations of 'prestige,' that all of us in the present-day world are coming to depend more and more on one another and are becoming increasingly necessary to one another."[60]
>
> February 1989: "In today's interrelated and increasingly integrated world, it is impossible to achieve progress in a society that is isolated from world processes by closed frontiers and ideological fences. This applies to any society, including socialist society. . . . Genuine socialism, in which the system serves the individual, not the other way around, can freely develop only in the context of interrelationships with the rest of the world."[61]

The influential heads of research institutes and think tanks are also discussing the shift to the conception of an interdependent world. For example, Oleg Bogomolov, director of the institute that studies the Socialist

Bloc economies, has stated, "Previously we reasoned: the worse for the adversary, the better for us, and vice versa. But today this is no longer true; this cannot be a rule anymore. Now countries are so interdependent on each other for their development that we have quite a different image of the solution to international questions. The worsening of the situation in Europe will not at all help the development of the Socialist Party of Europe."[62]

And Yevgeniy Primakov argues that the 27th Party Congress "corrected the distortion under which the confrontation of two world systems, the socialist and the capitalist, was regarded apart from their interdependence" on such issues as the environment, energy, disease, and the very concept of survival.[63]

Conclusion

The Soviets' view of the world and of the U.S.–Soviet competition is clearly changing. In their New Thinking they are now in the process of reevaluating a broad range of policies and potential costs, including reconsideration of the nature of security in the contemporary world; the U.S.–Soviet military competition; the dangers inherent in growing nuclear arsenals; the importance of cooperative solutions to regional and global problems; Soviet relations with Eastern Europe; Soviet activity in the Third World; human rights in the Soviet Union; market incentives in the Soviet economy; and the role of the Soviet economy in the international economic system of the twenty-first century. In every one of these areas, the Soviets are reaching conclusions that, if implemented, will have profound consequences for U.S.–Soviet relations.

It is important to understand that if the Soviets are pursuing cooperative and accommodative policies, they are doing so for Soviet interests. Soviet offers to reduce armaments and improve relations are not founded in altruism, but on the current Soviet calculation that a peaceful environment will offer better prospects for the Soviet reform program and other policies. But we should also recognize that the fact that such an environment is good for the Soviet Union does not automatically mean that it is bad for the United States.

Indeed, here is the very essence of the answer to the question "Can we end the Cold War?" The Soviets are stating, in effect, that they desire it, and that it is in the interests of both the Soviet Union and the United States. In the words of Richard H. Ullman, "Soviet objectives are real and concrete rather than ideological and transcendental."[64] The missing factor is our response: the expression of an American desire to work toward reducing tension and increasing cooperation and a statement of an American vision of our nation's role in a world free of domination by the Cold War ideology.

In the next chapter I will sketch out a Western response to Gorbachev's initiatives.

V

Western Responses to the Shift in the Soviet Position

Western reactions, particularly those of the United States, to Gorbachev's proposals for changes in East–West political and military relations—changes so dramatic, so revolutionary, as to literally imply a desire to end the Cold War—have been skeptical, unimaginative and very cautious.

Perhaps at this stage, only forty-eight months after Gorbachev came on the scene, that is to be expected. For forty years U.S. foreign policy and defense programs have been shaped largely by one major force: fear of, and opposition to, the spread of Soviet-sponsored Communism. It will require a leap of the imagination for us to conceive of our national goals—our role—in a world not dominated by the struggle between East and West.

In the immediate postwar years, Americans viewed

the world as composed of: a group of Western nations devastated by war; colonial nations in Africa and Asia straining for freedom; developing countries elsewhere struggling to advance; and all endangered by the two great Communist powers, China and the Soviet Union, whom we saw as determined to extend their hegemony across the globe.

In such a world the United States viewed itself as: a generous benefactor of the poor, a source of aid to the nations seeking to recover from the war, the protector of freedom and democracy everywhere, and the defender of all against the Communist threat. Fearing that threat, the United States developed a massive military force, forged alliances with nations of both North and South, and supplied economic and military assistance to anti-Communist regimes across the globe.

The opposition between East and West has continued to dominate the world political scene. Neither national policies nor international institutions have yet adjusted to the possibility of a termination of the Cold War. And neither national nor international leaders have yet conceived of the shape of the world that would result, or of how to catalyze movement toward it. The world of today is still organized to reflect the rivalry—indeed, the enmity—between the socialist and capitalist camps.

Before we can respond to Gorbachev, we need a vision of a world which would not be dominated by that enmity. It would not be a world without conflict, conflict between disparate groups within nations and conflict extending across national borders. Racial and ethnic differences will remain. Political revolutions will erupt as societies advance. Historical disputes over political boundaries will continue. Economic differentials among nations, as the technological revolution of the twenty-first century spreads unevenly across the globe, will increase.

In those respects the world of the future will not be different from the world of the past: conflicts within and between nations will not disappear. But how different that world would be if the superpowers agreed that (a) neither would seek to take advantage of such disputes to increase or extend its political or military power beyond its borders, and (b) their bilateral relations would be conducted according to rules of conduct which precluded the use of force.

No leaders of East or West, and no scholar so far as I know, has sketched out how the nations of East and West and North and South might relate to one another in such a world or how they could move toward it through a series of steps extending over a decade or more. I will try to do so, dealing first with political actions and later with changes in military forces. The division is artificial and I make it solely to facilitate discussion—in fact, the moves in one sphere will have a synergistic relationship to moves in the other. The two should proceed concurrently.

A New Political Regime

It is clear that in the twenty-first century, regardless of actions by the Soviet Union and the United States, relations among nations will differ dramatically from those of the postwar decades. In the postwar years the United States had the power—and to a considerable degree we exercised it—to shape the world as we chose. In the next century, whether or not the Cold War ends, that will not be possible. While remaining the world's strongest nation, we will live in a multipolar world and our foreign policy and defense programs must be adjusted to that reality.

We have already seen the rise of Japan. We must expect it to play a larger and larger role—exercising greater political power and assuming greater political and economic responsibility—on the world scene. The same can be said of Western Europe, which will take a giant step toward economic integration in 1992. From that is bound to follow greater political unity which will strengthen Europe's power in world politics.

And by the middle of the next century several of the countries of what we now think of as the Third World will have so increased in size and economic power as to be major participants in decisions affecting relations among nations.

Estimated Population in Millions

	1988	2050
China	1,070	1,700
India	800	1,600
Brazil	190	300
Nigeria	110	400
Total	2,170	4,000

	1988	2050
Soviet Union	285	400
Western Europe	330	305
United States	245	280
Japan	123	120
Total	*983*	*1,105*

If China were to achieve its economic goals for the year 2000, and if it were to move forward during the next fifty years at satisfactory but not spectacular growth rates, the income per capita of its approximately 1.7 billion people in 2050 would be equal to that of the British in 1965. Its total Gross National Product would approximate that of the United States, Western Europe or Japan, and would exceed that of the Soviet Union. These figures are, of course, highly speculative. I point to them simply to emphasize the magnitude of the changes which lie ahead and the need to begin now to adjust our goals, our policies and our institutions to take account of them.

In such a multipolar world, neither the United States nor the Soviet Union would be able to so completely dominate their respective spheres as at present. Nor would the advantages outweigh the costs, even if it were possible. With or without changes in relations between East and West the United States must prepare to re-position itself, politically, for a new role in a new world— a world which our children living today will not be able to avoid.

In the postwar years, many political leaders in both

East and West believed that the southern half of the planet offered opportunities for strategic advance (control of straits, establishment of naval bases, destabilization of unfriendly regimes) and economic advantage (access to raw-material sources, creation of new markets and expansion of investment opportunities). But both East and West are beginning to recognize that political instability in the South makes achievement of strategic advantage costly and uncertain. And the rising level of economic interdependence, accompanied by strong nationalistic forces, prevents achievement of long-term gains through attempts to control markets or raw-material sources. The effect of these changes on opportunities for and attempts at dominating the South by the North is just beginning to be reflected in geopolitical decisions. It surely is a factor influencing Gorbachev's plans; it should have an equal effect on our own. It points to the need for developing a new relationship both between East and West and between "the North" and the Third World.

At a minimum, such a relationship should (1) guarantee the military neutrality of the Third World; (2) commit the superpowers to sharp reductions in, and ultimately termination of, military support of conflicts between Third World nations and conflicts between opposition political parties within those nations; (3) assure support for a system of collective security for the nations of the South, and a mechanism for resolution of regional conflicts without superpower involvement; and (4) increase the flow of both technical and financial assistance to the developing countries to help them accelerate their rates of social and economic advance.

Agreement by East and West to support such a program not only would represent adjustment to the reality of economic and political change in the Third World, but would be consistent with moves to dampen down and ultimately terminate the Cold War. It would be a return to Roosevelt and Churchill's conception of the postwar world, a conception which, when first formulated in 1941 and later expanded into a proposal for establishment of the United Nations, was uncontaminated by the ideology of the Cold War.

Roosevelt and Churchill's Vision of Relations Among Nations in the Postwar World

Roosevelt and Churchill's vision of the postwar order began to take shape at their first meeting off the coast of Newfoundland aboard the cruiser *Augusta* on August 9–12, 1941. It was then that they signed the Atlantic Charter, stating that it set forth "certain common principles in the national policies of their respective countries on which they base their hopes for a better future for the world." The document stated:

1. The United States and United Kingdom seek no aggrandisement, territorial or other.
2. They desire to see no territorial changes that do not accord with the freely expressed wishes of the peoples concerned.

3. They respect the rights of all peoples to choose the form of government under which they will live; and they wish to see sovereign rights and self-government restored to those who have been forcibly deprived of them.

4. They will endeavor, with due respect for their existing obligations, to further the enjoyment by all States, great or small, victor or vanquished, of access, on equal terms, to the trade and to the raw materials of the world which are needed for their economic prosperity.

5. They desire to bring about the fullest collaboration between all nations in the economic field, with the object of securing for all improved labour standards, economic advancement, and social security.

6. They hope to see established a peace which will afford to all nations the means of dwelling in safety within their own boundaries, and which will afford assurance that all men in all the lands may live out their lives in freedom from fear and want.

7. Such a peace should enable all men to traverse the high seas and oceans without hindrance.

8. They believe that all the nations of the world, for realistic as well as spiritual reasons, must come to the abandonment of the use of force. Since no future peace can be maintained if land, sea, or air armaments continue to be employed by nations which threaten, or may threaten, aggression outside of their frontiers, they believe, pending the establishment of a wider and permanent system of general security, that the disarmament of such nations is essential. They will likewise aid and encourage all other practicable measures which will lighten for peace-loving peoples the crushing burden of armaments.

Recognizing the idealistic nature of the Atlantic Charter and the difficulty of applying its principles in particular situations, I nonetheless can think of no better expression of our national goals, hopes and aspirations for a post–Cold War world. We should accept it as such and consider how to apply it.

To implement the Atlantic Charter and to maintain postwar order, Roosevelt was increasingly attracted to the concept of an international organization. Negotiations among the Americans, the British and the Soviets by late 1943 had begun to include discussions of just such an institution. Roosevelt's conviction regarding the importance of the international organization had been solidified by 1944.

He reasoned that, in the past, American isolation and neutrality had failed to keep the peace. With no faith, therefore, in isolation, neutrality or balance-of-power arrangements, he saw no alternative to international cooperation. A Great Power conference was convened on August 21, 1944, at Dumbarton Oaks, to flesh out that concept. It led to the San Francisco Conference in April 1945 to frame the Charter of the United Nations. The document ultimately was signed on June 26, 1945.

Roosevelt's hopes for a strong, united organization that would defend a single interpretation of the postwar order were, of course, not to be fulfilled. By the time the United Nations was organized, East–West rivalry rendered it impotent.

But is it not time to return to Roosevelt's conception

of a world in which order would be maintained through international cooperation and support for a set of multilateral institutions—the United Nations and the regional organizations? To move toward realization of Roosevelt's vision, should not East and West agree on a Code of Conduct to cover relations between themselves and between them and other nations?

A Code of Conduct

An earlier attempt at establishing a U.S.–Soviet Code of Conduct, the 1972 Nixon-Brezhnev Basic Principles Agreement, was unsuccessful. Its failure was due, in part, to increased Soviet activism in the Third World in the mid- to late 1970s. The 1972 Basic Principles agreement was simply contradictory to the interests of at least one of its signatories, and no one realistically expected its terms to be obeyed.

Now, however, circumstances have changed, and a mutually beneficial Code of Conduct can perhaps be negotiated. Alexander L. George has written extensively on the advantages to be gained from—as well as the limits on—explicit rules of superpower behavior. He has argued that "the two superpowers should seek to develop, through timely, intensive discussions, a series of individual ad hoc understandings on how they would limit their competition and involvement in a particular country or region." George believes that even if the effort to devise the rules proves abortive or only partially successful, the interaction inherent in the effort itself can help clarify motivations, goals and perceptions.[1]

Perhaps more important, the Soviets are retracting a good many of their costly Third World commitments—the commitments that doomed the 1972 agreement to failure—and Gorbachev himself has suggested that "new rules of coexistence" might be drafted.[2]

Such "new rules" could provide that:

1. Each bloc's political interests will be pursued through diplomacy, not military threats or the use of force.

2. Consistent with number one, each bloc's military forces will be restructured to defensive postures and reduced to a balance at substantially lower levels.

3. The super powers will not become involved in regional conflicts.

4. The nations of East and West, and in particular the super powers, will utilize international organizations to solve regional and global problems, including conflicts within and between Third World nations.

The Code of Conduct would have precluded such unilateral postwar actions as Soviet intervention in Afghanistan, Angola (via the Cubans), Indochina (via the North Vietnamese) and Korea (via the North Koreans); U.S. intervention in Vietnam, the Dominican Republic, Nicaragua, Grenada and the Persian Gulf; and British and French intervention in Egypt.

Application of the Code

Applied to areas of potential conflict today, it might lead to the following actions by the United States and the Soviet Union:

1. Relations between Eastern and Western Europe.

The major risk of confrontation between East and West arises from the unresolved long-term relationship between Eastern and Western Europe. This must be addressed if the Cold War is to end. It is essential, therefore, that the European nations—particularly East and West Germany—be encouraged by both the United States and the Soviet Union to begin to formulate a long-term, stable relationship, a position to be reached within two or three decades. Gorbachev has begun to move in this direction with his proposal for a "common European home," a "Europe from the Atlantic to the Urals" united, not politically, but in common efforts to solve global and regional problems. He hasn't offered detailed plans for the construction of the "common house"—as initially conceived it appears to carry a sign "No Room for North Americans"—but neither we nor the Western Europeans have gone far in proposing alternatives. We should encourage the parties to do so. While they are engaged in that task, we should not make it more difficult by stimulating dissident elements in the Eastern Bloc to engage in civil disobedience.

2. Arab–Israeli Relations. The ultimate solution to the Middle East problem requires acceptance by the world, including Israel and the Palestine Liberation Organization, both of Israel's right to live in peace and of the rights of the Palestinians to a home on, and some form of self-government in, the West Bank. It is very likely that the start of negotiations to work toward such a solution would be facilitated by the convocation of an international conference backed by the United States and the Soviet Union.

3. Latin America. In general, the political unrest in Latin America, and particularly in Central America— e.g. in Nicaragua and El Salvador—has not been the result, in the first instance, of action by the Soviet Union or its proxy Cuba. Instead, it has been a function of the failure of the political elites in each nation to address the basic needs of the mass of their people. That failure often led to political disorder. After disorder developed, the Soviets, in accordance with Cold War behavior, intervened with military assistance—the United States often did the same. In the future, under the terms of the Code of Conduct, neither superpower would intervene. No longer would the Soviet Union, directly or indirectly, support efforts to subvert established governments in the hemisphere, and never again would the United States introduce military forces unilaterally. How, then, will political conflicts be resolved? They will continue to fester, as they have in Panama, unless the Latin-American nations themselves, through the Organization of American States—or through ad-hoc arrangements such as the Contadora and Arias plans—seek to bring peace to the area.

4. Apartheid in South Africa. For all too long, the United States failed to denounce Apartheid as strongly as our national traditions called for. We held back because we feared that such action would weaken the Afrikaaner government, and that that in turn would react to the advantage of the Soviets. Ultimately, we unilaterally imposed economic sanctions which have proven quite ineffective. In the future, in accordance with the Code of Conduct, we would seek to develop a consensus in the United Nations to deal effectively with the problem on a multilateral basis.

5. The Persian Gulf. There may again be disruption of petroleum traffic through the Persian Gulf. Should that occur, instead of unilaterally introducing the U.S. Navy, as we did in 1987, we should support the establishment of a UN force to assure safe passage of oil cargoes.

6. Supply of Arms to Third World Nations. The U.S. Foreign Aid program—totaling approximately $13 billion per year—is today largely a program of military assistance and defense support. Less than 25 percent of the total is supplied to the poorer nations of the world in the form of development assistance. The Soviet aid program is similarly oriented. In the future, both the

United States and the Soviet Union would stop delivery of offensive arms to Third World nations and would sharply cut back the flow of other forms of military assistance.

From the examples given above, it is clear that renouncement by the United States and the Soviets of unilateral action in the Third World will leave a vacuum. It can be dealt with only by strengthened regional and international organizations. Many of these organizations, in particular the OAS, have for years been moribund. They must be rebuilt to play a dominant role in resolving disputes among nations and within nations. Their crisis prevention and peace-keeping roles, which for forty years have suffered from lack of support—indeed, have faced direct opposition—from the United States and the Soviet Union, must be reorganized, restaffed and redirected.

While steps are being taken to reduce the danger of East–West political conflict, the arms-control negotiations now under way can be expanded in scope and accelerated in time.

An Expanded Arms-Control Agenda

The short-term arms-negotiation agenda, to be completed by the mid-'90s, should stress early completion of the START Treaty; rapid progress toward the restructuring and balancing of conventional forces in Europe at substantially lower levels; and, in association with the conventional-force adjustments, large reductions in tactical nuclear forces. A longer-term objective, to be realized perhaps by the end of the century, should be to sharply reduce dependence on nuclear weapons for deterrence of conventional-force aggression.

I'll discuss each of these subjects in turn.

The Current Negotiations

We are at a critical moment in the negotiations. The new Soviet leadership has given arms-reduction efforts the highest possible priority. But here in the United States the political consensus that led to successful ratification of the INF Treaty and support for START is severely threatened. I fear that the unresolved issues in the START Treaty and the mounting criticism of the arms-control negotiations, coming from many quarters, could cause this consensus to unravel.

Gorbachev has undeniably shown a boldness of vision, advocating sweeping measures to reverse the nuclear-arms race and reduce conventional arms in Europe. These bold proposals have been accompanied by remarkable flexibility at the negotiating table. The Soviets agreed to unequal reductions and extensive on-site inspection in the INF Treaty. And the framework of the START Treaty, calling for deep reductions in strategic arms, which the Soviets have agreed to, largely reflects U.S. concerns about Soviet advantages in ballistic missiles. In conventional arms, Gorbachev has not only proposed a three-phase plan for substantial cuts, but on December 7, 1988, announced major unilateral reductions.

Not long ago, in the days when Soviet officials were always rejecting U.S. proposals, Gorbachev's approach to diplomacy would have been unimaginable. Yet, now that the Soviet Union has a leader who, in the words of British Prime Minister Margaret Thatcher, is someone the West "can do business with," a great debate is brewing among experts here in the United States about whether and how to pursue arms reductions.

The U.S. opponents of START have developed a three-pronged attack. One group argues that pursuing START is dangerous because it will inevitably involve limiting our right to test and deploy strategic defenses. Others claim that reductions in strategic arms will erode the credibility of "extended deterrence," thereby increasing the chances of conventional aggression by the Soviets. A third group believes that START's specific reductions will leave U.S. nuclear forces more vulnerable than they are today.

Since the frequency and intensity of these criticisms may well grow as the negotiations continue, they merit careful examination.

START and Crisis Stability. The most important criticism of START relates to its effect on crisis stability. This is a valid—indeed, central—issue. The principal aim of arms control is not simply to reduce the number of weapons but to make nuclear war less likely by reducing incentives for either country to launch a

163

preemptive attack in a crisis. For the United States, this goal—of enhancing crisis stability—means ensuring the survivability of U.S. systems by curtailing the capability of Soviet forces and by encouraging a Soviet shift to a more stabilizing force posture.

The critics of START state it will increase the vulnerability of U.S. land- and sea-based systems. They point out that the number of submarines will decline from the present thirty-five to some sixteen to eighteen. The critics' mistake is to equate reduced numbers with reduced survivability. With or without START, it is planned to sharply decrease the number of submarines. We have decided that the increased range, quietness and efficiency of Trident as compared to Poseidon submarines justifies concentrating submarine-launched-ballistic-missile (SLBM) warheads in a smaller number of boats. There are simply no breakthroughs in anti-submarine warfare on the horizon that would make our Trident submarines vulnerable. Over time, if Soviet capabilities in this area were to improve dramatically, we are free under START to increase the number of submarines we deploy by reducing the number of weapons each one carries.

The issue that seems to generate a disproportionate share of controversy is the question of ICBM vulnerability. Some critics suggest START will make our fixed ICBMs more vulnerable because the number of U.S. silos may be reduced to a greater extent than the number of Soviet SS-18 warheads. Thus, critics claim that START will threaten crisis stability, since the ratio of

Soviet counterforce warheads to fixed U.S. ICBM targets would, in that case, rise.

This need not occur. The Scowcroft Commission, appointed by President Reagan, concluded, in a judgment which I share, that our current triad of land-, sea- and air-based strategic nuclear forces is invulnerable in the face of current and prospective Soviet forces. While our land-based missiles may become somewhat more vulnerable as Soviet systems are further modernized, START need not make the situation worse. On the contrary, unless we choose to deploy our forces under START in a greatly reduced number of fixed—as opposed to mobile—launchers, the critics' fears will not be realized. We can make the decision to do otherwise. Consequently, depending on the mix we choose of existing and modified Minuteman missiles, START can modestly or greatly diminish whatever Soviet incentives may exist to attack U.S. ICBMs.

START and Extended Deterrence. Perhaps the most troublesome of all the attacks on START is the one which seeks to make a connection between strategic-arms reductions and the likelihood of conventional war in Europe. Those who express such concerns propose that START be formally linked to improvements in the conventional balance. They claim that START would reduce the deterrent capability of our strategic nuclear forces. But I see no possible way in which this could occur. Because the reductions in START are so balanced and will enhance the overall survivability of U.S.

strategic forces, and because the United States would still retain nuclear weapons numerous enough and flexible enough to support NATO strategy, our capability to use nuclear forces in defense of Europe would remain unchanged. Therefore, whatever role strategic nuclear forces now play in deterring the threat of Soviet conventional aggression—and I regard that role as minimal—they would play an equal or greater role after they are adjusted to the treaty limits.

To hold START hostage to a conventional-arms-control agreement is tantamount to postponing it indefinitely. While the opportunity to achieve conventional-arms reductions is, I believe, greater today than ever before, the extreme complexity of the subject matter makes it abundantly clear that actual progress will take many years.

START and SDI. A major unresolved issue standing in the way of agreement on START is the status of the Strategic Defense Initiative (SDI), the anti-ballistic missile system proposed by President Reagan. My opposition to this program is well known. I believe it poses grave risks far out of line with any possible benefits.

Those risks include: its enormous waste of resources, which, depending on the choice of system, may be measured in the hundreds of billions of dollars; the fact that it will initiate an arms race in outer space and fuel the competition in strategic arms on earth; and the possibility that it would increase the temptation for preemptive attack in a period of crisis.

Meanwhile, the potential benefits of SDI are minimal. Given the enormous destructive power of nuclear weapons, no defense in the foreseeable future, no matter how extensive and costly, can protect the population of the United States. This vulnerability is not a policy choice but a grim fact of life in the nuclear age.

Despite the grave risks and minimal benefits, proponents of the SDI insist on keeping alive its test and development program, which they hope and expect will lead to deployment of the system in the mid-1990s. They are unwilling to recognize that neither the Soviets nor the United States will or should accept a limitation on strategic offensive weapons if the opponent is permitted an unlimited defense. Former Secretary of Defense Caspar Weinberger has gone so far as to propose recently that the United States withdraw from the ABM Treaty. And yet the inextricable link between reductions in strategic offensive arms and restrictions on strategic defenses remains as true today as it was in the late 1960s and early 1970s when the ABM Treaty was first formulated. I know that the Joint Chiefs of Staff who advised me in the 1960s shared this view. I would be very surprised if the current Joint Chiefs do not still share it. If the Chiefs were pressed whether they could support deep reductions in U.S. strategic forces, such as those START would require, combined with an unlimited Soviet deployment of a nationwide defense, I can't imagine they would say yes.

The U.S. and Soviet governments must find a way to finesse this impasse over missile defense. If the

United States insists that strategic defense be given free rein, we cannot expect the Soviet Union to implement arms reductions, nor should we in the United States be willing to do so. The best solution would be for the new Administration to endorse the traditional interpretation of the ABM Treaty, to heed the bipartisan advice offered by six previous Secretaries of Defense—three Republicans, Melvin R. Laird, Elliot L. Richardson and James R. Schlesinger, and three Democrats, Clark M. Clifford, Harold Brown and myself. We stated that limiting the testing and deployment of both U.S. and Soviet strategic defenses through the ABM Treaty is critical to U.S. security and "makes possible negotiation of substantial reductions in strategic offensive forces."[3]

Alternatively, the impasse could be overcome through Soviet action. Recognizing that Congress has not permitted the President to conduct SDI tests that go beyond the traditional interpretation of the ABM Treaty, the Soviets could make a unilateral statement to the effect that their national interests would be jeopardized by U.S. actions inconsistent with the ABM Treaty. The right of a nation to alter its legal obligations under a treaty like START because of a threat to its national interest is well established. The United States would be hard pressed to justify opposition to such an expression of sovereignty.

Those who oppose START because it will involve limits on strategic defenses are correct in their assumption, but incorrect in their conclusion. Obtaining deep reductions in Soviet ballistic-missile forces in exchange for restrictions on a program of such dubious value and potentially dangerous consequences is an offer we should be delighted to accept.

I do not believe that any leg of this "triad of opposition" to START will stand up under careful scrutiny. However, if these attacks continue, they will certainly be divisive. They could yet prove to be decisive, and this historic opportunity would be missed or substantially deferred.

A Golden Opportunity for Conventional-Arms Reductions. Turning to conventional arms, NATO and Warsaw Pact countries have been discussing conventional weapons for some fifteen years. These talks have yielded essentially no progress. The problem has been that the Soviet Union holds significant numerical advantages in key categories of weaponry. To redress the numerical imbalance requires confronting and evaluating deep asymmetries between East and West in geography, weapons quality and force requirements. For example, the massive Soviet army in Eastern Europe in addition to its military role has always had a political one—to guarantee Soviet domination of Eastern Europe.

But the negotiating landscape has dramatically changed. Gorbachev's bold proposals to sharply cut conventional arms are based on his stated willingness to reshape Soviet conventional forces to achieve "reasonable sufficiency" as opposed to superiority, and to adopt a "defensive" rather than an offensive posture. And, apparently recognizing that the Warsaw Pact retains two to three times as many tanks, artillery pieces and attack helicopters as NATO does, Gorbachev has also said he is willing to make asymmetrical, as opposed to equal, reductions to common levels.

It is not yet clear what Gorbachev means by the term "reasonable sufficiency" or the words "defensive posture." Nor is it obvious what force changes "asymmetrical reductions" would translate into. But it is in our interest to seize this opportunity to explore the seriousness and content of Gorbachev's statements. We often complain that his deeds fail to match his words. But the force reductions he announced at the United Nations on December 7, 1988—a cut of 500,000 in military personnel and major cuts as well in tanks, artillery and aircraft—are clear evidence of his desire to move to a nonaggressive defensive posture. That action alone substantially reduces the danger of a successful attack by the Warsaw Pact.

A successful conventional-arms agreement would be one of the great diplomatic triumphs in this century. Not only would it stabilize the military confrontation in Europe at sharply lower force levels, but it would signal, as well, the beginning of an historic geopolitical transformation of Europe.

Negotiation of a conventional-force agreement will be immensely complex. The participation of many nations—all sixteen members of NATO must be involved—is always a complicating factor. In addition, the subject matter does not lend itself to simple formulas as in the case of nuclear arms. And verification of such an agreement will involve difficult trade-offs. So the sooner NATO formulates a comprehensive response to Gorbachev's initiative the better.

Tactical Nuclear-Force Modernization and the German Problem. Another related and potentially divisive issue in the near term is the future of NATO's short-range nuclear forces. Gorbachev has said he wants to negotiate the reduction and elimination of nuclear forces with ranges below five hundred kilometers. Meanwhile, the Alliance has concluded that in light of the apparent Soviet advantage in conventional arms, short-range nuclear forces should not be discussed at this point. Instead, it is developing proposals to modernize and improve those forces.

One of the unfortunate consequences of the INF Treaty is the effect it has had on the Federal Republic of Germany. Rightly or wrongly, Germans across the political spectrum feel "singularized": they are beginning to recognize that many, if not most, of the remaining nuclear weapons under NATO's control not only are stationed on German soil but are also designed to explode on German soil. This strongly held belief has made it very difficult to reach a consensus on force modernization. So far, the dispute has been papered over. Certainly it will come to the fore if a decision to modernize the Lance system (a tactical nuclear missile deployed in Germany) is finalized and deployment plans are announced.

Even though I view linkage as a dangerous strategy, the linkage between negotiated reductions in NATO tactical nuclear forces and movement toward improving the conventional balance seems unavoidable under present circumstances. However, I hope that we fully explore the opportunity to use arms reduction rather than an arms buildup to improve the situation.

In recent years I have publicly questioned the wisdom of NATO's threat to use nuclear weapons first in response to conventional aggression by the Soviet Union. Nevertheless, as long as we maintain this policy, our modernization efforts should focus on weapons which raise—not lower—the nuclear threshold. This means deemphasizing nuclear artillery shells, because these weapons create powerful pressures on field commanders to "use them or lose them," which in turn increases the likelihood of early first use. Similarly, to the extent that modernization is deemed necessary, it should emphasize survivable systems.

Several years ago the concept of unilateral arms-control measures was often discussed. More recently, as the U.S. and Soviet governments have achieved some success in bilateral negotiations, this concept has faded from view. While we must and will continue to negotiate arms-control agreements, I believe that the whole quesiton of the military confrontation in Europe lends itself well to unilateral measures—by both East and West. Gorbachev's announcement on December 7, 1988, is an illustration of what can be done.

The anxiety in the Federal Republic of Germany, while certainly not a new phenomenon, is one which

NATO can help dispel by a unilateral move. We now have some sixteen hundred nuclear artillery shells in Europe. A unilateral withdrawal of, at a minimum, one thousand of these weapons could ease German concerns and would be desirable in and of itself, given the danger of unintended escalation these weapons present in a military conflict.

It should even be possible to move toward reductions in defense budgets through "concerted" unilateral actions. For example the United States could state that it planned to move gradually, over a five-year period, to reduce defense expenditures if the Soviet Union did likewise. Recognizing the impossibility of precise verification of the absolute amount of expenditures, national means of surveillance, nonetheless, should permit determination of the trend. At any time either party could change its plan if it was not satisfied the other was performing in accordance with the stated objective. Such an approach was initiated while I was Secretary of Defense in the 1960s. After showing initial promise, it collapsed in the face of the incremental outlays associated with the Vietnam buildup.

Unilateral actions, such as those I have described, are not only desirable in and of themselves. They would also serve to catalyze the bilateral arms-control negotiations. And the prospect for reductions in conventional arms could be improved further by agreement on confidence-building measures, beyond those already contained in the Stockholm Agreement, to reduce each side's fear of a surprise attack.

The Longer-Term Objectives of Nuclear-Arms Negotiations

The "short-term " program—completing the START negotiations, achieving a balance of conventional forces in Europe, reducing the number of tactical nuclear weapons and strengthening confidence-building measures—will greatly improve crisis stability. However, after it is completed, NATO and the Warsaw Pact will retain thousands of nuclear warheads, and NATO's strategy will continue to be based on first use of these weapons under certain circumstances. The danger of nuclear war—the risk of destruction of our society—will have been reduced but not eliminated. Can we go further? Surely the answer must be yes.

More and more political and military leaders are accepting that major changes in NATO's nuclear strategy are required. Some are going so far as to state that our long-term objective should be to return, insofar as practical, to a nonnuclear world. Illustrative of the changes in thinking which are now under way was this statement by the former Chancellor of the Federal Republic of Germany, Helmut Schmidt, in 1987: "Flexible response [NATO's current strategy calling for the use of nuclear weapons] is nonsense. Not out of date but nonsense, because it puts at risk the lives of sixty million Germans and some fifteen million Dutch and I don't know how many million Belgian people and others who live on Continental European soil. The Western idea—which was created in the 1950s—that we should be

174

willing to use nuclear weapons first, in order to make up for our so-called conventional deficiency, has never convinced me. I can assure you that after the use of nuclear weapons on German soil, the war would be over as far as the Germans go, because they would just throw up their hands. To fight on after nuclear destruction of your own nation has started is a very unlikely scenario, and you need to be a mathematician or a military brain to believe such nonsense."[4]

Similar views have been expressed by a number of NATO military experts:

Field Marshal Lord Carver, Chief of the British Defense Staff from 1973 to 1976, is totally opposed to NATO's ever initiating the use of nuclear weapons. He has said, "At the theater or tactical level any nuclear exchange, however limited it might be, is bound to leave NATO worse off in comparison to the Warsaw Pact, in terms both of military and civilian casualties and destruction."[5]

General Johannes Steinhoff, the former Luftwaffe Chief of Staff, stated, "I am firmly opposed to the tactical use [of nuclear weapons] on our soil."[6]

Admiral Noel A. Gayler, former Commander in Chief of U.S. ground, air and sea forces in the Pacific, wrote: "There is no sensible military use of any of our nuclear forces."[7]

Melvin Laird, Secretary of Defense in the Nixon Administration, shares the views of the military commanders. He said, "These weapons are useless for military purposes."[8]

Such diverse groups and individuals as the U.S. Catholic bishops, Henry Kissinger and antinuclear advocates have all stated that nuclear deterrence is an untenable strategy which the U.S. public will not support indefinitely.

And President Reagan repeatedly asserted that a nuclear war cannot be won and must never be fought—assertions which clearly imply disavowal of NATO's current strategy of flexible response. His proposal for the Strategic Defense Initiative went even further and had as its objective the complete elimination of all nuclear weapons.

In spite of such statements, many NATO security experts—I would say most—have not yet been willing to support a basic change in NATO's nuclear strategy. For example, with reference to a proposal for eliminating nuclear weapons, Zbigniew Brzezinski, President Carter's national-security adviser, said, "It is a plan for making the world safe for conventional warfare. I am therefore not enthusiastic about it."[9]

But two developments in the years ahead are likely to lead to a shift in such judgments: Restructuring of conventional forces in Europe into defensive postures, at levels that are clearly in balance, will sharply reduce the justification for the nuclear-deterrent force. And arms negotiations which result in nuclear forces of equal capabilities—forces with which neither side could win a nuclear war—will remove the deterrent capability of the force. Such "no-win" strategic-force structures are implicit in the proposed START agreements.

If it were decided to move away from nuclear deterrence, how would this be done?[10]

Mikhail Gorbachev has proposed that the United States and the Soviet Union aim at achieving the total elimination of all nuclear weapons by the year 2000. But the genie is out of the bottle—we cannot remove from men's minds the knowledge of how to build nuclear warheads. Therefore, unless technologies and procedures can be developed to ensure detection of any steps toward building a single nuclear bomb by any nation or terrorist group—and such safeguards are not on the horizon—an agreement for total nuclear disarmament will almost certainly degenerate into an unstable rearmament race. Thus, despite the desirability of a world without nuclear weapons, an agreement to that end does not appear feasible either today or for the foreseeable future.

However, if NATO, the Warsaw Pact and the other nuclear powers were to agree, in principle, that each nation's nuclear force would be no larger than was needed to deter cheating, how large might such a force be? Policing an arms agreement that restricted each side to a small number of warheads is quite feasible with present verification technology. The number of warheads required for a force sufficiently large to deter cheating would be determined by the number any nation could build without detection. I know of no studies which point to what that number might be—they should be initiated—but surely it would not exceed a few hundred, say at most five hundred. Very possibly it would be far less, perhaps in the tens.

Such an agreement could be achieved only over a period of years—say by the year 2000—but should we not set it as our ultimate objective and lay out a series of steps to move toward it?

The Budgetary Impact

As we progress through the arms control agenda, the U.S. defense budget could be reduced substantially. It might well be possible, within six to eight years, to cut military expenditures in half in relation to GNP—i.e., to 3 percent. That would make available, in 1989 dollars and in relation to 1989 GNP, $150 billion per year to be divided between additional personal consumption and the financing of the pressing human and physical infrastructure needs of both our own and Third World societies. It would go far toward assuring that U.S. industry would be in the lead in the technological world of the twenty-first century. Lest it be thought a U.S. defense budget of 3 percent of GNP is a fantasy, we should remember that today Japan's defense expenditures are 1 percent of GNP, Canada's 3 percent, and the average of all NATO nations', excluding the United States, 3 percent.

The political actions and arms-control proposals which I have outlined in this chapter on Western responses to Soviet initiatives should be supplemented by measures of economic and environmental cooperation and by scientific and cultural exchanges. All would be designed to integrate the Soviet Union more fully into our increasingly interdependent global order. Each action could be taken independently of the others. But together they would exert a powerful synergistic effect which would indeed make the whole greater than the sum of its parts. But are there not risks associated with such a Western response? I turn next to that subject.

VI

Potential Criticisms of a Program to End the Cold War

After forty years, an attempt to shift relationships between East and West as dramatically as is implied by the words "a Program to End the Cold War" is by its very nature uncertain of accomplishment, potentially risky, and likely to be highly controversial.

Among the criticisms which might be directed against it are the following:

1. A respite in the Cold War will strengthen the Soviets, and they will use their increased strength to weaken the West.

2. To date, with the exception of Gorbachev's December 7, 1988, announcement at the United Nations, there is little evidence of major changes in Soviet military doctrine or defense forces.

3. Moves to terminate the Cold War will undermine support both in Europe and in the United States for defenses sufficient to provide security during the negotiating process.

4. There will always be conflicts of interest—political, economic and military as well as ideological—between nations, and especially between Great Powers, which cannot be resolved by goodwill alone. Therefore, while the United States should welcome and encourage any sign of liberalization in the Soviet Union, it should never confuse such changes with a Soviet abandonment of basic foreign-policy aims. It is naive to think otherwise.

5. Past experience indicates that the Soviets will not adhere to agreements to reduce political tensions or to limit arms. At times that are advantageous to the USSR, it will attempt to "break out" of such agreements. Its ability to do so is greater than ours because of the nature of its political system.

6. Gorbachev is likely to fail. If he fails, his successor will reverse Gorbachev's policies, placing a complacent West in a position of inferiority.

Each of these criticisms is worthy of consideration, but each can be rebutted:

1. Were the Soviet Union to strengthen its domestic economy, it might indeed direct that strength against the West. However, it will be years, perhaps even dec-

ades, before Perestroika begins to yield significant economic benefits. The reforms will bring huge disruptions of production and people. Gorbachev himself has said the reform process will take a generation. In the intervening period the relative economic strength of the West is bound to increase. Moreover, achievement of Perestroika will require that the USSR be integrated into global markets and international scientific exchanges. The integrating process itself will contribute to a lowering of political tensions between East and West and will tend to make the changes irreversible.

2. It is correct to say that with the exception of Gorbachev's December 7, 1988, announcement there has been little change in Soviet military doctrine or defense forces. The concepts Gorbachev has put forward, "reasonable sufficiency," "defensive posture" and "asymmetrical reductions," are new to the East as well as to the West. While eminently sound, they are difficult to translate into particulars. So difficult that neither the United States nor NATO has been able to respond to Gorbachev's general proposals with a comprehensive bill of particulars as to how they should be implemented. Until we do so, criticism of his inaction is hardly justified.

3. Maintaining public support in the United States and Europe for appropriate defense budgets will be difficult in any event. The requirement to reduce the U.S. fiscal deficit has already led to propsals to cut defense expenditures in real terms. These pressures will, in turn, lead to suggestions that Europe and Japan shoulder a larger part of our common defense burden. This

they are unlikely to do in any way that would permit a significant cut in our defense budget. So public support for defense expenditures will erode. But I believe it will erode less rapidly if we appear to be trying to maintain a strong, stable defense posture as a foundation for moving in a constructive way to probe the degree to which we can reduce political tension between East and West.

4. Many historians will assert that Great Powers— and, regardless of the success of Perestroika, the Soviet Union will clearly remain a Great Power—always have sought and always will seek an external enemy; they need such a target both to justify their military force and to maintain the power of the internal ruling class. History tends to support that judgment. But, as I pointed out in Chapter V, the world of the twenty-first century will be different from that of any other period since the dawn of civilization. For the first time, no nation and no group of nations will be able to stand alone economically, technologically, environmentally, politically or militarily. Attempts by the Soviet Union to do so not only would endanger international peace and carry great risks for the USSR, but would be doomed to failure in the long run. Therefore, our objective, as I will discuss more fully below, should be to remain so secure as to make an effort by any nation to move away from interdependence toward domination so costly as to be unattractive.

5. On the whole, Soviet compliance with arms-control agreements has been good. General Chain, now Commander of the Strategic Air Command, told Congress during the height of the debate over Soviet non-

compliance with SALT, "If you take the body of the [arms-control] treaties in a macrosense, they have complied with the large majority of the treaties." The one notable exception is the Krasnoyarsk radar, which appears to be a clear violation of the ABM Treaty, probably as a result of bureaucratic bungling. However, our diplomatic protests over construction of the radar are beginning to bear fruit, as the Soviets have stopped work on it and have offered to tear it down. In all cases of noncompliance, even if the military balance has not been affected, we should insist on strict adherence to the treaty, and we should, and can, maintain the capability to initiate appropriate countermeasures if the response is not satisfactory.

6. It is probably correct to say that the majority of U.S. Soviet experts believe Gorbachev will fail. Marshall Goldman, associate director of the Russian Research Center at Harvard University, expressed this sentiment when he said, "I think Gorbachev has about a year left."[1] At least some Soviet leaders are also pessimistic. Andrey Sakharov, for example, has said, "Perestroika is at a very sharp, acute phase."[2] However, while Gorbachev undoubtedly faces difficulties, there is mounting evidence that the top Soviet political leadership, and the majority of the Soviet intelligentsia, recognize he has diagnosed properly the basic problems faced by their society. They understand there is no alternative to his political and economic reforms if long-term economic crises and resultant political disorders are to be avoided. If Gorbachev's efforts fail—and they may—his successor will face the same problems. To solve them he will

be required ultimately to introduce the same solution. There may be steps forward and steps back, but for the next decade or two it is likely the Soviet Union will move in the general direction laid down by the General Secretary.

The review of potential criticisms of attempts to dampen down and ultimately to terminate the Cold War indicates that even under the best of circumstances the way will not be smooth and progress may indeed be slow and interrupted. Can we protect ourselves against an even less desirable outcome, a collapse of Perestroika both nationally and internationally and a resumption of political conflict and military confrontation?

I believe the answer is clearly Yes.

As nuclear-arms agreements bring reductions in nuclear forces and add to crisis stability, there need never be a weakening of our nuclear deterrent. Concurrently with the changes in nuclear forces, it appears likely that, through both unilateral actions and bilateral agreements, the present numerical superiority of Warsaw Pact conventional forces will be reduced. In addition, there is a high probability that we can agree on confidence-building measures which will greatly reduce the danger to each side of surprise attack.

Together these actions should give the West high confidence that we can move down a path which provides hope for terminating the Cold War without incurring unacceptable risks in the event we fail to achieve that objective.

VII

An Approach to the Twenty-first Century

I began this essay by pointing out that the Cold War between East and West—a continuing series of political crises, any one of which had the potential for escalating to military confrontation carrying the risk of destruction of our civilization—has existed for nearly forty years.

It has led to huge U.S. defense expenditures; it has turned our attention away from urgent domestic problems; it has distorted our relations with other nations; and it has moved us away from our traditional values.

It is inconceivable to me that we should be content to continue on the present path of East–West confrontation for another forty years. The risks of military conflict, with disastrous consequences, are unacceptably high, and the dangers of erosion of public support for our present policies are increasingly great. We do have an opportunity—the greatest since the end of World War II—to formulate and seek to establish a new relationship. We can do so from a position of strength. If our hopes are not realized we will have lost nothing. If we succeed, we can enter the twenty-first century with a far more stable political relationship between East and West, and with a totally different military strategy: one of mutual security instead of war-fighting; with vastly smaller nuclear forces, no more than a few hundred weapons in place of fifty thousand; with conventional forces in balance and in defensive rather than offensive postures; and with a dramatically lower risk that our nation will be destroyed by unintended conflict.

With such a change in East–West relations, the long-term outlook for the United States will be brighter than at any time in this century.

As a nation, we are in the forefront of the technological revolution. We have the largest common market in the world—a union of fifty states, in effect a union of fifty nations. We possess a flexible, skilled labor force (albeit one which requires large investments in continuing education and training); strong capital markets; adventuresome entrepreneurs; and stable political institutions. With these strengths, the United States is uniquely situated to move into the twenty-first century as the strongest of the nations in a multipolar world in which there will be a far lower risk of war between the great power blocs.

It is true, as Paul Kennedy says, that in the twenty-first century the relative power of the United States will be less. But no nation will have greater power. And in absolute terms we can be far stronger than today: economically, politically and psychologically. There need, then, be no divergence, as there has been in recent years, between our ideals—our belief in representative government, individual liberty, economic and social advance for all peoples—and our international behavior. If we are bold—if we dare break out of the mind-sets of the past four decades—we can help shape international institutions, as well as relations among nations, in ways which will lead to a far more peaceful world and a far more prosperous world, for the peoples of East and West and North and South.

Notes

Chapter I

1. Western Cold War scholars can be divided into three
   schools: the "traditionalist" or "orthodox," the "revision-
   ist" and the "postrevisionist." The traditionalists—for example, Herbert Feis—tend to believe that Soviet foreign
   policy was affected very little by any outside influence,
   that the Soviet Union was internally driven to occupy
   and control Eastern Europe, and that, in many ways, the
   "blame" for the Cold War can be placed on Moscow. The
   revisionists—most notably William Appleman Williams
   and Gar Alperovitz—emphasize that the United States
   played a major role in shaping Moscow's foreign policy,
   and they appear to believe that, in large measure, U.S.
   policies fueled the suspicion and hostility of the Cold
   War. The postrevisionists—best exemplified by William
   Taubman—have found the truth somewhere in between.
   They claim, as I will, that both the United States and

the Soviet Union were guilty of errors of judgment and perception. Since both states were defending legitimate security interests in a period of great flux, a certain amount of conflict was inevitable, but it was exacerbated by poor information, a dearth of expertise, and excessive suspicion. The Soviet official view has long been that the West was wholly responsible for the rise and exacerbation of superpower tension in the postwar era, but Moscow has recently permitted a new line to be publicized. For example, in an article, "We Are All in the Same Boat," published in the popular and important Soviet weekly *Literaturnaya Gazeta* of March 1, 1989, the Soviet historian Nikolai Popov argued that Joseph Stalin should bear a large portion of the blame for launching the Cold War. In a dramatic break with past Soviet practice, Popov stated that it was reasonable for the West to equate the Soviet Union under Stalin with Hitler's Germany as two "totalitarian colossi." (For an analysis of the article, see Michael Dobbs, "Soviet Historian Blames Cold War Start on Stalin," *Washington Post,* March 3, 1989, p. A32.)

Popov makes an important and often overlooked point. He cautions his Soviet readers that the negative views of the Soviet Union held by many in the West are founded on accurate perceptions of the Soviet past. Although the Soviet public is only now learning of Stalin's crimes and atrocities, knowledge of the purges and killings has long been widespread in the West. Popov argues that the West's negative perceptions of the Soviet Union stem from "revulsion against Stalinism." He goes on to say: "We must see our country through the eyes of the rest of the world," and he argues, ". . . For prewar Europe and the United States, our country was, above all, a country of bloody enforced collectivizations, mass repressions and camps, a country of terror and dictatorship, the country of Stalin." An open discussion of this sort in the Soviet Union—an airing of the view that Stalin and the Soviets bear a portion of the blame for the origin and evolution of the Cold War—is a tardy but extremely welcome development.

2. Herbert Feis, *Churchill, Roosevelt, Stalin: The War They Waged and the Peace They Sought* (Princeton: Princeton University Press, 1967), pp. 448–49.

3. A. W. DePorte, *Europe Between the Superpowers: The Enduring Balance* (New Haven: Yale University Press, 1979), p. 87.

4. *Ibid.*, p. 59.

5. I am grateful to Allen Lynch for this point. For a detailed treatment of the issue, see his forthcoming *The Soviet Study of International Relations* (Cambridge University Press), especially the introduction.

6. Vojtech Mastny, *Russia's Road to the Cold War: Diplomocy, Warfare and the Politics of Communism, 1941–1945* (New York: Columbia University Press, 1979), pp. 283, 306, cited in William Taubman, *Stalin's American Policy from Entente to Détente to Cold War* (New York: W. W. Norton, 1982), p. 8.

7. DePorte, p. 69.

8. Barton J. Bernstein, "Confrontation in Eastern Europe," in Thomas G. Paterson, ed., *The Origins of the Cold War*, 2nd ed. (Lexington, Mass.: D. C. Heath and Co., 1974), p. 97.

9. *Ibid.*, pp. 97–98.

10. John Lewis Gaddis, *The United States and the Origins of the Cold War: 1941–1947* (New York: Columbia University Press, 1972), pp. 95–102.

11. For details on the "Morgenthau plan" and the other areas of dispute, see Gaddis, pp. 95–132, and Adam B. Ulam, *Expansion and Coexistence: Soviet Foreign Policy, 1917–73* (Holt, Rinehart and Winston, 1974), pp. 390–94.

12. DePorte, p. 72. Emphasis in original.

13. Ulam, p. 437.

14. DePorte, pp. 136–37.

15. X, "The Sources of Soviet Conduct," *Foreign Affairs*, originally published in June 1947, reprinted in Vol. 65, No. 4 (Spring 1987), p. 856.

16. *Ibid.*, p. 857.

17. *Ibid.*, p. 858.

18. *Ibid.*, p. 864.

19. *Ibid.*, p. 866.

20. *Ibid.*, p. 867.

21. George F. Kennan, "Containment Then and Now," *Foreign Affairs*, Vol. 65, No. 4 (Spring 1987), p. 887.

22. A. G. Mileykovsky, ed., *International Relations After the Second World War* (Moscow, 1962), p. 376, cited in Ulam, *Expansion and Coexistence*, p. 437.

23. Taubman, p. 176.

24. *Ibid.*

25. *Ibid.*, p. 177.

26. DePorte, pp. 104–5.

27. Taubman, p. 199.

28. Alexander Deconde, *A History of American Foreign Policy*, Vol. II, 3rd ed. (New York: Charles Scribner's Sons, 1978), pp. 246–47.

29. George F. Kennan, *The Nuclear Delusion: Soviet–American Relations in the Atomic Age* (New York: Pantheon Books, 1982), p. 36.

30. Marian Irish and Elke Frank, *U.S. Foreign Policy: Con-*

text, Conduct, Content (New York: Harcourt Brace Jo-
vanovich, 1975), pp. 459–60.

31. Gregg Herken, *The Winning Weapon: The Atomic Bomb
    in the Cold War, 1945–1950* (New York: Knopf, 1980),
    p. 222.

32. *Ibid.*, p. 271.

33. Cited in Michio Kaku and Daniel Axelrod, *To Win a
    Nuclear War: The Pentagon's Secret War Plans* (Boston:
    South End Press, 1987), p. 63.

34. Herken, pp. 318–19.

35. Kennan, *The Nuclear Delusion,* p. 35.

36. Taubman, p. 231.

37. Ulam, p. 546.

38. Ibid. p. 565.

Chapter II

1. Adam Ulam, *Expansion and Coexistence: Soviet Foreign
   Policy, 1917–73* (New York: Holt, Rinehart and Winston, 1974), p. 577.

2. *Report to the President: United States Policy Toward
   the Soviet Satellite States in Eastern Europe*, NSC 58/
   2, Dec. 8, 1949, cited in Lincoln Gordon, *Eroding Empire: Western Relations with Eastern Europe* (Washington, D.C.: Brookings Institution, 1987), p. 71.

3. Ulam, p. 614.

4. For evidence on China, see H. W. Brands, Jr., "Testing
   Massive Retaliation: Credibility and Crisis Management
   in the Taiwan Strait," and Gordon H. Chang, "To the
   Nuclear Brink: Eisenhower, Dulles and the Quemoy-
   Matsu Crisis," both in *International Security*, Vol. 12,

No. 4 (Spring 1988). For a discussion of the general issue, see Mark A. Pekala, "The Effect of Nuclear Weapons on World Order Since 1945: Can Peace Among the Nuclear States Last Forever?" an unpublished paper delivered at the New Faces Conference conducted by the Arms Control Association and the International Institute for Strategic Studies, in Bellagio, Italy, June 1988.

5. Ulam, p. 620.

6. Quoted in Robert V. Daniels, "Doctrine and Foreign Policy," in Erik P. Hoffmann and Frederic J. Fleron, Jr., eds., *The Conduct of Soviet Foreign Policy* (New York: Aldine Publishing Co., 1980), p. 162.

7. *Documents on International Affairs*, 1961, p. 33.

8. See also my *Blundering into Disaster: Surviving the First Century of the Nuclear Age* (New York: Pantheon Books, 1987), pp. 6–8. For a more detailed treatment, see Jack M. Schick, *The Berlin Crisis, 1958–1962* (Philadelphia: University of Pennsylvania Press, 1971), pp. 147–73.

9. Ulam, p. 656.

10. John F. Kennedy, "Toward a Strategy of Peace," commencement address at the American University, Washington, D.C., June 10, 1963, in Young Hum Kim, ed., *Patterns of Competitive Coexistence: USA vs. USSR* (New York: Capricorn Books, 1966), pp. 421–23.

11. *New York Times*, Sept. 28, 1966, p. 14, cited in Robert C. Tucker, "United States–Soviet Cooperation: Incentives and Obstacles," in Hoffmann and Fleron, p. 306.

12. "On the International Situation and the Foreign Policy of the Soviet Union," *Pravda*, June 28, 1968.

13. Harry Gelman, "Rise and Fall of Détente," *Problems of Communism*, Vol. XXXIV, No. 2 (March–April 1985), p. 52.

14. Raymond L. Garthoff, *Détente and Confrontation: American–Soviet Relations from Nixon to Reagan* (Washington, D.C.: Brookings Institution, 1985), pp. 69–70.

15. Henry A. Kissinger, *The White House Years* (Boston: Little, Brown, 1979), p. 266.

16. Gelman, pp. 52–53.

17. Garthoff, p. 29.

18. *Ibid.*, p. 74.

19. *Ibid.*, p. 37.

20. Colonel D. Proektor, interview in *La Stampa* (Rome), Nov. 7, 1979, cited in Garthoff, pp. 57–58.

21. George F. Kennan, *The Nuclear Delusion: Soviet–American Relations in the Atomic Age* (New York: Pantheon Books, 1982), pp. 42–43.

22. William Taubman, *Stalin's American Policy: From Entente to Detente to Cold War* (New York: W. W. Norton, 1982), p. 237.

23. Quoted in Gerard Smith, *Doubletalk, the Story of SALT I* (Garden City NY: Doubleday, 1980), p. 177.

24. Kennan, p. 43.

25. *Ibid.*

26. Gelman, p. 58.

27. *Ibid.*, p. 54.

28. Garthoff, pp. 1068–89.

29. Donald Zagoria, "Into the Breach: New Soviet Alliances in the Third World," in Hoffmann and Fleron, p. 499.

30. *Ibid.*, pp. 495–96.

31. *Ibid.*, p. 496.

32. Garthoff, p. 563.

33. Taubman, p. 239.

34. Cited in Hedrick Smith, "Russia's Power Strategy," in Hoffmann and Fleron, p. 744.

35. Garthoff, p. 1078.

36. *Public Papers of the Presidents of the United States, 1981*, p. 57.

37. President Reagan's Florida speech to the convention of the National Association of Evangelicals, March 8, 1983, *Public Papers of the Presidents of the United States, 1983*, p. 363.

38. "Statement by Yu. V. Andropov, General Secretary of the Central Committee of the Communist Party of the Soviet Union, Chairman of the Presidium of the Supreme Soviet of the USSR," *Pravda*, Sept. 29, 1983.

Chapter III

1. From an unpublished statement by Sir Brian Urquhart (University of Texas Lectures).

2. John Steinbruner has often emphasized this point.

3. See my *Blundering into Disaster: Surviving the First Century of the Nuclear Age* (New York: Pantheon Books, 1987), pp. 5–6.

4. Helmut Schmidt, *Defense or Retaliation?* (New York: Praeger, 1962), p. 101.

5. Solly Zuckerman, *Nuclear Illusion and Reality* (New York: Viking, 1982), pp. 70–71.

6. The text of the U.S. bishops' pastoral letter, "The Challenge of Peace: God's Promise and Our Response," appears in *Origins*, Vol. 13, No. 1.

Chapter IV

1. *Mikhail Gorbachev's Answers to Questions Put by Time Magazine* (Moscow: Novosti, 1985), p. 5.

2. Mikhail Gorbachev, *Political Report of the CPSU Central Committee to the 27th Party Congress* (Moscow: Novosti, 1986), p. 72.

3. *Ibid.*, p. 74. Emphasis in original.

4. Gorbachev, *Perestroika: New Thinking for Our Country and the World* (New York, Harper and Row, 1987), pp. 140–41. Emphasis in original.

5. *Ibid.*, p. 219.

6. Dec. 7, 1988, speech to UN, *New York Times,* Dec. 8, 1988, p. A16.

7. Lead editorial, "A Concrete Program for Assuring Peace and Security," *Voyennaya Mysl* (Military Thought), No. 6 (June 1986), pp. 3–4, cited in Raymond L. Garthoff, "New Thinking in Soviet Military Doctrine," *Washington Quarterly,* Summer 1988, p. 134.

8. Gorbachev, *Political Report . . .*, p. 74.

9. TASS press release, July 28, 1986.

10. *Izvestiya,* Aug. 19, 1986.

11. *Pravda,* Feb. 17, 1987.

12. *Ibid.*, Sept. 17, 1987.

13. *New York Times,* Sept. 25, 1987, p. A8.

14. *Ibid.*, Oct. 16, 1987.

15. *Los Angeles Times,* Sept. 4, 1988, p. 4.

16. Gorbachev, *Perestroika,* p. 165.

17. Speech in Prague, April 1987, *Washington Post,* Oct. 12, 1987, p. A30.

18. *Ibid.,* Oct. 13, 1987, p. A15.

19. Richard H. Ullman, "Ending the Cold War," *Foreign Policy* 72, p. 136.

20. Robert Legvold and the Task Force on Soviet New Thinking, *Gorbachev's Foreign Policy: How Should the United States Respond?,* Foreign Policy Association Headline Series, No. 284 (Washington, D.C., 1988), pp. 15–16.

21. Alexey Izyumov and Andrey Kortunov, "The Soviet Union in the Changing World," *International Affairs* (Moscow), August 1988, pp. 52–55.

22. See the *New York Times* and *Washington Post* reporting on March 7, 1989.

23. For further discussion of this point, see Mark A. Pekala, *Gorbachev's Speech to the United Nations: A New Vision of World Politics and Major Military Cutback,* Issue Brief No. 13 (Washington, D.C.: The Committee for National Security, Dec. 9, 1988).

24. These figures and further discussion are found in Rob Leavitt, *Update: Warsaw Pact Military Reductions and Reforms* (Tempe, Ariz.: Operation Real Security), February 1989. See also Army General P. Lushev, "In the Interests of a Durable Peace," *Krasnaya zvezda,* March 3, 1989, p. 3.

25. "Mikhail Gorbachev Meets with American Artists, Intellectuals and Scientists at the Soviet Embassy" and "Mikhail Meets with U.S. Businessmen," *Soviet Life,* Special Supplement on the Washington Summit, n.d., pp. 6 and 17–18.

26. Esther B. Fein, "Hebrew Teaching in Russia Seen As Means to Win West," *New York Times,* Nov. 4, 1988, p. A8.

27. *Ha'aretz* (Tel Aviv), March 2, 1989, p. 3, translated in Foreign Broadcast Information Service (FBIS) *Daily Report: Soviet Union,* March 8, 1989, p. 63.

28. Gorbachev, *Political Report* . . . .

29. Gorbachev, *Perestroika,* p. 13.

30. *Pravda,* April 24, 1985.

31. Aleksandr Bovin, "*Perestroika* and the Fate of Socialism," *Izvestiya,* July 11, 1987.

32. *Pravda,* April 8, 1985.

33. April 10, 1985, TASS report on Gorbachev's meeting with Thomas P. "Tip" O'Neill, Speaker of the U.S. House of Representatives.

34. Gorbachev, *Perestroika,* pp. 146–49.

35. *Pravda,* Feb. 17, 1987.

36. Feb. 18, 1988, speech to the CPSU Plenum, *Moscow News,* No. 9 (3309), 1988, Supplement, p. 6, and speech to the UN, Dec. 7, 1988, *New York Times,* Dec. 8, 1988, p. A16.

37. "Firmly Following the Course of Renewal," *Pravda,* March 2, 1989, translated in FBIS *Daily Report: Soviet Union,* March 3, 1989, p. 56.

38. "Gorbachev's Modernization Program: A Status Report," paper presented by CIA and DIA for submission to the Subcommittee on National Security Economics of the Joint Economic Committee, March 19, 1987, p. 1.

39. "Speech by Mikhail Gorbachev, General Secretary of the CPSU Central Committee, at the Plenary Meeting of the CPSU Central Committee on February 18, 1988," *Moscow News,* No. 9 (3309), 1988, Supplement, p. 4.

40. Abel Agenbegyan and Timor Timofeyev, *The New Stage*

of Perestroika (New York: Institute for East–West Security Studies, 1988), p. 40.

41. Gorbachev, *Perestroika*, p. 21.

42. *Nineteenth CPSU Conference: Documents and Materials* (Moscow: Novosti, 1988), p. 9.

43. *New York Times*, Feb. 28, 1988.

44. "Gorbachev's Modernization Program: A Status Report," p. 4.

45. Seweryn Bialer, "Gorbachev's Move," *Foreign Policy* 68, p. 60, and Ed A. Hewett, *Reforming the Soviet Economy: Equality versus Efficiency* (Washington, D.C.: The Brookings Institution, 1988), p. 325.

46. "A New Philosophy of Foreign Policy," *Pravda*, July 10, 1987.

47. *Mikhail Gorbachev's Answers to Questions Put by Time Magazine* (Moscow: Novosti, 1985), p. 24.

48. Speech at the Moscow international peace forum, reported in FBIS *Daily Report: Soviet Union*, Feb. 17, 1987, p. AA17.

49. Gorbachev, *Political Report . . .*, p. 74.

50. Speech on extending Soviet unilateral moratorium on testing, FBIS *Daily Report: Soviet Union*, Aug. 19, 1986, p. AA1.

51. *Pravda*, Feb. 17, 1987.

52. Gorbachev, *Perestroika*, pp. 12–13.

53. Gorbachev speech on the 70th anniversary of the Bolshevik Revolution, Nov. 2, 1987, *October and Perestroika: The Revolution Continues* (Moscow: Novosti, 1987), pp. 64–65.

54. Gorbachev's Dec. 10, 1987, press conference after the

Washington summit, *Soviet Life* supplement cited in Note 25, p. 24.

55. October 1987 speech in Murmansk, TASS press release, Oct. 5, 1987.

56. Gorbachev's Dec. 10, 1987, press conference after the Washington summit, *Soviet Life* supplement cited in Note 25, p. 31.

57. Gorbachev toast to Reagan, May 30, 1988, Moscow, TASS press release, May 31, 1988.

58. TASS dispatch, Feb. 23, 1989, press release from the Information Dept., Soviet Embassy, Washington, D.C.

59. From an April 10, 1987, speech in Prague, *For a "Common European Home," For a New Way of Thinking* (Moscow: Novosti, 1987), p. 20.

60. Gorbachev, *Perestroika*, p. 137.

61. TASS dispatch, Feb. 23, 1989, press release from the Information Dept., Soviet Embassy, Washington, D.C.

62. Interview on Czechoslovak TV, FBIS *Daily Report: Soviet Union*, April 16, 1987, p. F2.

63. "A New Philosophy of Foreign Policy," *Pravda*, July 10, 1987.

64. Richard H. Ullman, "Ending the Cold War," *Foreign Policy* 72, pp. 144–45.

Chapter V

1. See his "The Search for Agreed Norms," in Graham T. Allison and William Ury, eds., with Bruce J. Allyn, *Windows of Opportunity: From Cold War to Peaceful Competition in U.S.–Soviet Relations* (Cambridge, Mass.: Ballinger Publishing Co.,1989), pp. 45–66.

2. Gorbachev, "The Reality and Guarantees of a Secure World," *Pravda* and *Izvestiya*, Sept. 17, 1987.

3. Letter to President Reagan from Ambassador Gerard C. Smith, March 9, 1987.

4. An interview on BBC Radio with Stuart Simon, July 16, 1987.

5. London *Sunday Times*, Feb. 21, 1982.

6. Hans Günther Brauch, "The Enhanced Radiation Warhead: A West German Perspective," *Arms Control Today*, June 1978, p. 3.

7. *Congressional Record*, 97th Congress, 1st Sess., July 17, 1981 (Washington, D.C., 1981), p. S7835.

8. Melvin R. Laird, "What Our Defense Really Needs," *Washington Post*, April 12, 1982.

9. John J. Fialka and Frederick Kempe, "US Welcomes Soviet Arms Plan, but Dismisses Part as Propaganda," *Wall Street Journal*, Jan. 17, 1986.

10. See my *Blundering into Disaster: Surviving the First Century of the Nuclear Age* (New York: Pantheon Books, 1987), pp. 122–24.

Chapter VI

1. *International Herald Tribune*, Feb. 11, 1989.

2. *Washington Post*, Nov. 8, 1988.

Acknowledgments

Public television recently aired a program entitled "The Education of Robert S. McNamara." It is an accurate description of the focus of my life during the past three decades.

The process began in December 1960, when President-elect Kennedy asked me to serve in his cabinet as Secretary of Defense. At that time, I had little experience in either foreign affairs or security issues. I had taught at the Harvard Graduate School of Business Administration as an assistant professor, served in the U.S. Army in World War II as a lieutenant colonel, and, a short time before, been elected president of Ford Motor Company. It was hardly a background that qualified me for the position Kennedy offered. After I pointed this out, he remarked he wasn't aware of any school for Presidents either. So I accepted. But it was with the clear understanding—an agreement from which he never once deviated—that I would staff the upper echelons of the department with the brightest and most experienced people I could find, without regard to partisan political considerations.

That is how there came to be assembled the ablest group of individuals to serve together in a single government department in the history of our republic. They included Steve Ailes, Robert Anthony, Colonel George Brown, Harold Brown, William Bundy, Joseph Califano, John Connally, Alain Enthoven, John Foster, Eugene Fubini, Roswell Gilpatric, William Gorham, Morton Halperin, Charles Hitch, Paul Ignatius, William Kaufmann, Tom Morris, Russell Murray, David McGiffert, John McNaughton, Paul Nitze, Colonel Robert Pursley, Stan Resor, Harry Rowen, Jack Ruina, Cyrus Vance, Paul Warnke, Adam Yarmolinsky, Herb York and Eugene Zuckert.

They, along with my key military advisers—in particular Generals Maxwell Taylor, Earle G. Wheeler and Lyman L. Lemnitzer—and my colleagues in the State Department and the National Security Council tutored me and laid the foundation for my thinking in international affairs. I draw on that experience to this day.

For help on this small volume I am enormously grateful to Mark Pekala and Jane Wales. They assisted me in planning and carrying out the research on which it is based. James Rubin, of the Arms Control Association, was particularly helpful in bringing me up-to-date on the status of the arms negotiations.

The text, in whole or in part, was reviewed by a number of scholars and security experts, including Norman Birnbaum, William Carmichael, Peter Kaufman, George Kennan, Allen Lynch, William Miller, Robert Pastor, George Rathjens, John Steinbruner, Peter Tarnoff, Brian Urquhart, Paul Warnke and Adam Yarmolinsky. Their stimulating comments—and, at times, harsh criticism—forced me to reexamine both my premises and my conclusions. They of course bear no responsibility for the final product, but I owe all of them my thanks.

Miss Jeanne Moore, my never-complaining secretary, worked nights and weekends through innumerable drafts and changes to produce the final text.

Index

211

INDEX

INDEX

NATO (*cont.*)
  nuclear threat and, 97, 98,
    99, 103, 166, 171–77
Nazi Germany, Soviet Union
  compared with, 84
Nehru, Jawaharlal, 78
Neto, Agostinho, 79
new political regime, 149–61
  Code of Conduct for, 156–61
  population factors and, 150–
    151
  Roosevelt's and Churchill's
    view of postwar order and,
    153–56
New Thinking in Soviet policy,
  108–44
  applied to Eastern Europe
    and the Third World, 115–
    118, 119–21
  economic restructuring and,
    108, 123–24, 129–30
  in foreign and defense pol-
    icy, 118–23
  geopolitical objectives and,
    108, 115–18
  human rights and, 108, 124–26
  Marxist-Leninist ideology
    and, 108, 126–30
  reassessment of security re-
    quirements and, 108–14
  summary of, 108
  Western responses to, *see*
    Western responses to shift
    in Soviet position
New Thinking in Soviet policy,
  origins of, 130–43
  Central Committee plenum
    and, 134–37
  Gorbachev's early efforts
    and, 133–34
  interdependence of nations
    and, 141–43
  nuclear threat and, 131,
    137–41
  Soviet economy and, 131–32

Nicaragua, 83, 157, 159
Nixon, Richard M., 70–72, 74,
  81, 127, 156
Nixon Doctrine, 71–72, 77
Nkrumah, Kwame, 78
North American Defense Command, 81
North Atlantic Treaty (1949),
  42, 46
North Atlantic Treaty Organization, *see* NATO
North Korea, 43–45, 157
North Vietnam, 79, 157
  U.S. bombing of, 71
Norway, 43
NSC-68, 43, 47, 48
nuclear nonproliferation treaty
  (1968), 66
nuclear war:
  Chinese view of, 60
  increased Soviet attention to
    risk of, 131, 137–41
  threat of, as Cold War cost,
    96–102
nuclear weapons, 58, 63–67
  arms-control agenda and,
    162, 171–78, 188
  of China, 58
  first strike capacity and, 46, 47
  German problem and, 171–75
  Gorbachev's views on, 110,
    111, 138–39
  longer-term objectives of ne-
    gotiations on, 174–78
  moral costs of, 102–4
  NATO and, 84, 97, 98, 99,
    103, 166, 171–77
  parity and, 72
  proliferation of, 58, 97

Organization of American
  States (OAS), 159–60, 161

Pakistan, 58, 68
  U.S. aid to, 82–83

218

INDEX